TELL ME WHICH?

CHANCELLOR
❧ PRESS ❧

An Hachette UK Company
www.hachette.co.uk

First published in 2002 by Chancellor Press,
a division of Octopus Publishing Group Ltd
Carmelite House, 50 Victoria Embankment,
London EC4Y 0DZ
www.octopusbooks.co.uk

Paperback edition 2010
This edition published in 2014 by Chancellor Press,
a division of Octopus Publishing Group Ltd

Copyright © Octopus Publishing Group Ltd 2002, 2010, 2014

All rights reserved. No part of this work may be reproduced or utilized
in any form or by any means, electronic or mechanical, including
photocopying, recording or by any information storage and retrieval system,
without the prior written permission of the publisher.

ISBN: 978-0-7537-2785-0

A CIP catalogue record for this book is available from the British Library

Printed and bound in China

5 7 9 10 8 6

CONTENTS

Planet Earth, 4

The Natural World, 36

History, 82

Science and Technology, 112

The Human Body, 142

The Solar System, 178

PLANET EARTH

CONTENTS

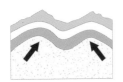

WHICH FIVE PARTS MAKE UP THE EARTH?   6
WHICH IS EARTH'S HIGHEST MOUNTAIN?   7

WHICH IS THE LARGEST ACTIVE VOLCANO ON EARTH?   8
WHICH IS THE WORLD'S LARGEST INACTIVE VOLCANO?   9

WHICH IS EARTH'S LARGEST HOT DESERT?   10
WHICH PARTS OF THE WORLD HAVE SAVANNAS?   11

WHICH PLACE ON EARTH IS THE HOTTEST?   12
WHICH PART OF THE WORLD HAS THE LEAST RAINFALL?   13

WHICH IS THE WORLD'S LARGEST OCEAN?   14
WHICH PLACE ON EARTH IS THE DEEPEST?   15

WHICH PHENOMENON CAUSES TIDES?   16
WHICH ACTIVITY CAUSES OCEAN CURRENTS?   17

WHICH PHENOMENON CAUSES A TSUNAMI?   18
WHICH PROCESS CREATES A HURRICANE?   19

WHICH HEMISPHERE DO YOU LIVE IN?   20
WHICH DAY OF THE YEAR IS THE SHORTEST?   21

WHICH PROCESS STARTS THE WATER CYCLE?   22
WHICH PROCESS CAUSES ACID RAIN?   23

WHICH AREAS OF THE WORLD ARE MOST SUSCEPTIBLE TO FLOODING?   24
WHICH IS EARTH'S LONGEST RIVER?   25

WHICH PROCESS CREATES A GLACIER?   26
WHICH PROCESS SHAPES THE COAST?   27

WHICH PROCESSES CAUSE EROSION?   28
WHICH PROCESSES CAUSE DEFORESTATION?   29

WHICH ROCKS ARE MADE UP OF LAYERS?   30
WHICH ROCKS USUALLY HAVE VISIBLE CRYSTALS?   31

WHICH ROCKS ARE METAMORPHIC?   32
WHICH ARE THE MAIN TYPES OF FOSSIL FOUND ON EARTH?   33

WHICH FOSSIL FUEL ORIGINATED IN THE CARBONIFEROUS PERIOD?   34
WHICH OF EARTH'S PLANTS ARE THE OLDEST?   35

WHICH FIVE PARTS MAKE UP THE EARTH?

The Earth is a big ball, or sphere, made mostly of rock and has five main parts. The first is the atmosphere. This is the gaseous envelope that surrounds the solid body of the planet. The second is the hydrosphere. This is the layer of water that, in the from of oceans, covers approximately 71% of the planet's surface. The outside of the Earth is the third part. This is a crust of rock, called the lithosphere, and is about 16 to 48 km (10 to 30 miles) thick. The high parts of this crust are the continents, and the low parts of it hold the waters of the oceans, seas and lakes. The fifth part, deep inside the planet is Earth's core – a ball of iron and nickel. Between this central ball and the rocky crust is the fourth part, a shell about 3,200 km (2,000 miles) thick called the mantle.

FACT FILE

At 3.2 km (2 miles) below the surface of the Earth, the temperature is high enough to boil water. At the core, the temperature is believed to be as high as 5537.7°C (10,000°F).

WHICH IS EARTH'S HIGHEST MOUNTAIN?

The Earth's highest mountain is Mount Everest, which stands at 8,850 m (29,000 ft) tall. It can be found in the Himalayas, a mountain range in Asia, which is home to the ten highest mountain peaks in the world. Mountains are formed when the Earth's tectonic plates move. As layers of rocks push against each other, they buckle and fold at the edges. Mountains are pushed up at upfolds, and valleys are formed in downfolds. Another way that mountains can form is when the Earth's crust cracks on a fault. Layers of rock on one side of the crack can be pushed up to form a mountain. Some mountain peaks stand alone high above the surrounding landscape, but most mountains – like Mount Everest – are joined together to form a range. When several ranges of mountains are grouped together, they are called a chain.

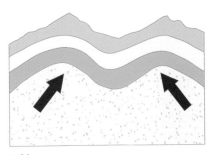

Fold mountain

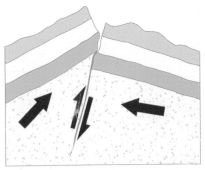

Fault mountain

FACT FILE

Mountain peaks are often seen to be surrounded by layers of cloud. This is because as winds laden with water are blown towards the mountains, they are forced to rise and the temperature drops. The water condenses into clouds at these higher altitudes.

WHICH IS THE LARGEST ACTIVE VOLCANO ON EARTH?

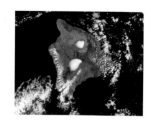

A volcano is an opening in the Earth's crust through which molten lava, red-hot rocks, steam and fumes pour out. An active volcano is one that erupts regularly or has the capacity to erupt. They are sometimes called dormant if they have not erupted for a very long period. The largest active volcano on Earth is Mauna Loa. Its base spreads over 50% of the island of Hawaii. Mauna Loa's summit is 9 km (5.6 miles) from the ocean floor and scientists estimate that its great mass is actually squashing the ocean floor down by another 8 km ((5 miles), giving the volcano a total height of just under 17 km (10.6 miles) from seafloor base to summit. The last time it erupted was in 1984.

FACT FILE

The Earth's crust is cracked into huge pieces that are constantly moving by just a few centimetres each year. The cracked sections, called tectonic plates, are supported by the oozing, soft rocks of the mantle beneath the Earth's crust. The unstable borders between the plates are known as 'rings of fire'. These are danger zones for both volcanoes and earthquakes.

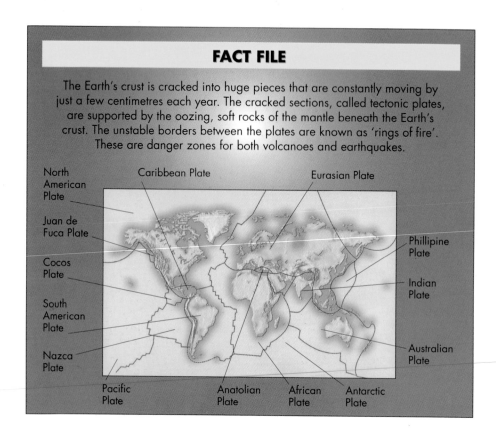

North American Plate

Caribbean Plate

Eurasian Plate

Juan de Fuca Plate

Phillipine Plate

Cocos Plate

Indian Plate

South American Plate

Nazca Plate

Australian Plate

Pacific Plate

Anatolian Plate

African Plate

Antarctic Plate

WHICH IS THE WORLD'S LARGEST INACTIVE VOLCANO?

The world's largest inactive volcano is on the island of Maui in Hawaii and is called Haleakala. It rises to a height of about 3,055 m (10,025 ft). Its crater is about 32 km (20 miles around and some 829 m (2,720 ft) deep. Like earthquakes, volcanoes mainly occur along fault lines. Molten rock, gases and ash are forced out through a gap in the Earth's crust to release the pressure that has built up. When there is very little pressure the volcano can remain in a dormant state for many, many years. It is not known whether Haleakala is extinct or dormant. The word dormant actually means 'sleeping'. So when people talk about a volcano being dormant, it really means it is temporarily sleeping and might erupt at any time in the future. An extinct volcano is one that will not become active again and will therefore not erupt again.

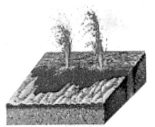

Fissure eruptions release liquid lava

Eruptions with less fluid lava form a low cone

Violent eruptions eject solid lava

FACT FILE

A major volcanic eruption can hurl boulders high into the air. These boulders, called volcanic bombs, can be very large indeed.

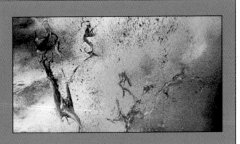

WHICH IS EARTH'S LARGEST HOT DESERT?

The world's largest hot desert is the Sahara in northern Africa. It stretches from the Atlantic Ocean in the west to the Red Sea in the east. As well as the sand dunes that people associate with deserts, it also has high,

rocky plateaux, mountains and areas of semi-desert. The only water apart from minimal seasonal rainfall is found in oases and in the river Nile, which flows through the desert.

Today, people live around the edge of the desert and some live at or travel between the oases, but thousands of years ago when it was wetter, people also lived in the desert's interior and many of their cave and rock paintings – called petroglyphs – have been found. An oasis is a fertile patch in a desert, which surrounds a water hole. This water comes from underground wells or springs. The Sahara has about 90 large oases, where there is enough water for people to live in villages and grow crops.

FACT FILE

Because a desert is defined by the amount of rainfall or snowfall it receives, the largest desert in the world is, in fact, the icy continent of Antarctica.

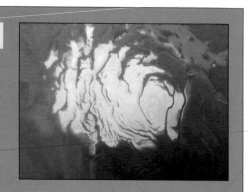

WHICH PARTS OF THE WORLD HAVE SAVANNAS?

FACT FILE

A wide variety of animals live on savannas – zebras, antelopes, rodents, birds, reptiles and insects.

Most savannas, also spelled savannahs, can be found in the tropics and lie between deserts and rain forests. A savanna is a grassland with widely scattered trees and shrubs. They cover more than two-fifths of Africa and large areas of Australia, India, and South America. They occur in regions that have both rainy and dry seasons.

The growth of trees on savannas is limited by the dry season, which may last for up to five months. When the dry season begins, grasses stop growing and turn brown, and most trees shed their leaves. Only the most drought-resistant trees can survive the climate here. Most savanna grasses grow in clumps. Acacias, baobabs, and palms are some common savanna trees.

WHICH PLACE ON EARTH IS THE HOTTEST?

There are several places on Earth that have recorded extreme temperatures. The hottest shade temperature was in Libya in 1922, when the temperature in the Sahara desert reached 58°C (136.5°F). Temperatures nearly as high as this were recorded in Death Valley in the United States in 1913. And the longest heatwave recorded was in Marble Bar, Australia, when the temperature stayed above 38°C (100.5°F). It lasted for 162 days from 23 October 1923 to 7 April 1924. The coldest ever recorded temperature was in Antarctica in 1983, when Russian scientists measured a temperature low of −89.2°C (−128.5°F).

FACT FILE

Over millions of years the human body has altered to suit the climate of the regions people inhabit. In general the hotter the region, the darker the skin of its inhabitants.

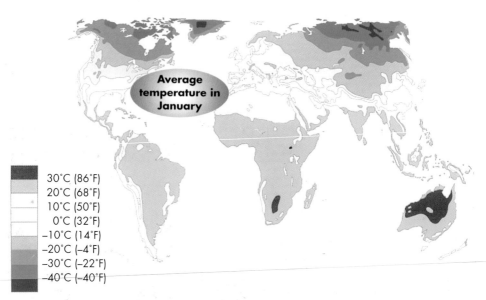

Average temperature in January

30°C (86°F)
20°C (68°F)
10°C (50°F)
0°C (32°F)
−10°C (14°F)
−20°C (−4°F)
−30°C (−22°F)
−40°C (−40°F)

WHICH PART OF THE WORLD HAS THE LEAST RAINFALL?

The Atacama desert, which lies between the Andes and the Pacific Ocean, is recognized as the driest place in the world. The Atacama desert remains so dry because it lies in a region where there is constant high air pressure, with little air movement, and with few clouds overhead, and that means hardly any rainfall. The longest drought in recorded history took place in this desert, in Calama, northern Chile. Beginning in 1571, no rain fell in the area for four whole centuries. It was not until 1971 that rainfall was first recorded again.

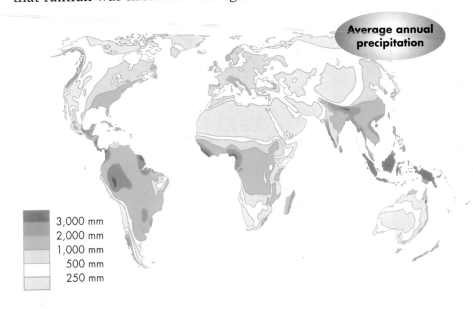

Average annual precipitation

3,000 mm
2,000 mm
1,000 mm
500 mm
250 mm

FACT FILE

Some people believe that animals are good predictors of weather. One such belief is that if cows are standing in their field, then dry weather is expected. If they are lying down, however, rain is expected.

WHICH IS THE WORLD'S LARGEST OCEAN?

The Pacific Ocean is the largest and the deepest of the world's five oceans. It covers more than one-third of the Earth's surface and contains more than half of its free water. It is sometimes divided into two nominal sections: the part north of the equator is called the North Pacific; the part south of the equator, the South Pacific. The name Pacific, which means peaceful, was given to the ocean by the Portuguese navigator Ferdinand Magellan in 1520.

The Pacific Ocean is the oldest of the existing ocean basins, its oldest rocks having been dated at around 200 million years. The Pacific Ocean is bounded on the east by the North and South American continents; on the north by the Bering Strait; on the west by the Asian continent, the Malay Archipelago, and Australia; and on the south by Antarctica.

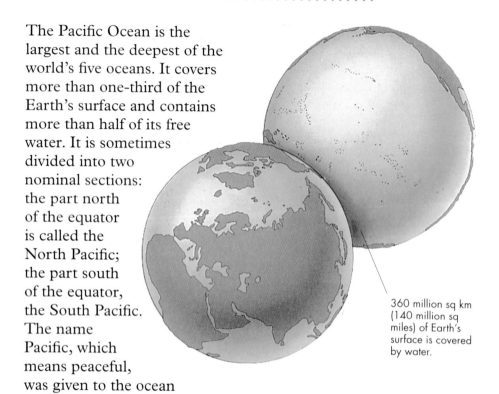

360 million sq km (140 million sq miles) of Earth's surface is covered by water.

FACT FILE

The Pacific Ocean contains more than 30,000 islands; their total land area, however, amounts to only one-quarter of 1% of the ocean's surface area.

WHICH PLACE ON EARTH IS THE DEEPEST?

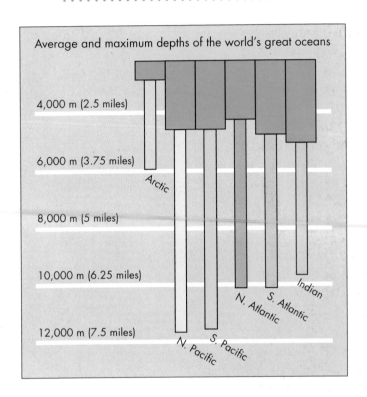

Average and maximum depths of the world's great oceans

4,000 m (2.5 miles)

6,000 m (3.75 miles)

Arctic

8,000 m (5 miles)

10,000 m (6.25 miles)

Indian

S. Atlantic

N. Atlantic

12,000 m (7.5 miles)

N. Pacific

S. Pacific

The deepest places on Earth are trenches in the oceans. Many trenches occur in the Pacific Ocean, especially in its western portion. Most trenches are long, narrow and deep, 3 to 4 km (2 to 2.5 miles) below the surrounding seafloor. The greatest depth anywhere in the ocean is found in the Mariana Trench southeast of Japan. It plunges more than 11 km (6.8 miles) below sea level. Frequent earthquakes and volcanic eruptions occur along the ocean trenches.

FACT FILE

For centuries, most people assumed that the cold, black depths of the ocean supported little or no life. Scientists have since discovered a great variety of living things in the deep sea.

WHICH PHENOMENON CAUSES TIDES?

The daily rise and fall of the ocean's tides occur because of the pull of gravity of the Moon. As the Earth spins round, the water in the oceans is 'pulled' towards the Moon slightly, making a bulge. There is a corresponding bulge on the other side of the Earth. Wherever the bulges are positioned it is high tide. In between, the water is shallower and so it is low tide. High tides occur every 25 hours, because at the same time that the Earth is spinning on its axis, the Moon is travelling around the Earth once every 27½ days. This means that high tides are one hour later every day.

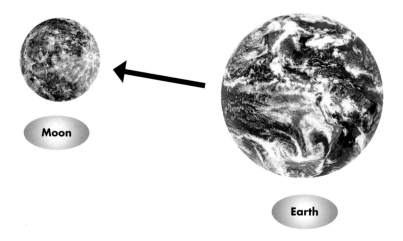

Moon

Earth

FACT FILE

Spring tides are tides with unusually high ranges twice per month when the Sun, Earth, and Moon are in line. They can be especially high in the spring and autumn.

WHICH ACTIVITY CAUSES OCEAN CURRENTS?

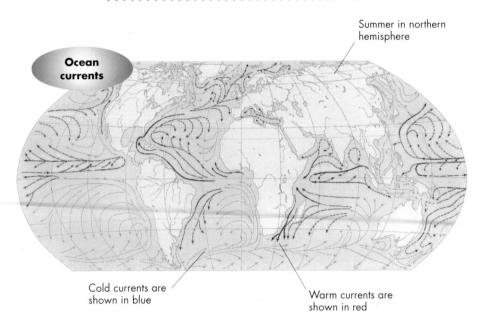

Ocean currents

Summer in northern hemisphere

Cold currents are shown in blue

Warm currents are shown in red

FACT FILE

A whirlpool is a mass of water that spins around and around rapidly and with great force. It may occur when opposing currents meet. It may also be caused by the action of the wind.

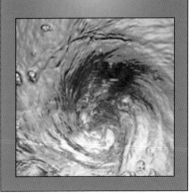

The ocean waters are moved by the wind on their surface and by movements within the ocean itself. Ocean currents are the result. Currents transfer heat around the Earth as they move and thus play a part in climate control. The spinning of the Earth dictates the way the water circulates. In the northern hemisphere it moves clockwise and in the southern hemisphere, anti-clockwise. Ocean currents vary in the summer and winter and a change in wind direction can change the current, influencing the weather in a particular country. A cold ocean current makes the weather colder and a warm one, warmer.

WHICH PHENOMENON CAUSES A TSUNAMI?

Also known as seismic sea waves, tsunamis are large, destructive waves caused by earthquakes on the ocean floor. When an earthquake happens, it gives a tremendous push to the surrounding seawater, and this creates the waves. Tsunamis may build to heights of more than 30 m (100 ft) when they reach shallow water near shore. In the open ocean, tsunamis typically move at speeds of 800 to 970 km (500 to 600 miles) per hour. They can travel great distances while diminishing little in size and can flood coastal areas thousands of miles from their source. In 2004, the Indian Ocean Tsunami killed hundreds of thousands of people and destroyed the coastline.

FACT FILE

Probably the best-known gauge of earthquake intensity is the local Richter magnitude scale, developed in 1935 by US seismologist, Charles F Richter.

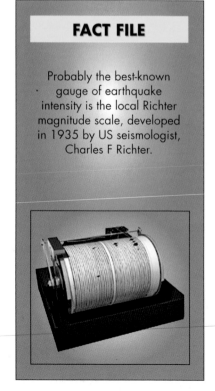

WHICH PROCESS CREATES A HURRICANE?

FACT FILE

The end of a hurricane comes quickly if a hurricane moves over land, because it no longer receives heat energy and moisture from warm tropical water.

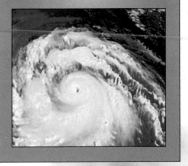

Hurricanes are caused by storms. A storm achieves hurricane status when its winds exceed 118 km (74 miles) per hour. By the time a storm reaches hurricane intensity, it usually has a well-developed eye at its middle. Surface pressure drops to its lowest in the eye. In the eyewall (or the eye of the storm), warm air spirals upwards, creating the hurricane's strongest winds. The speed of the winds in the eyewall is related to the diameter of the eye. Just as ice skaters spin faster when they pull their arms in, a hurricane's winds blow faster if its eye is small. If the eye widens, the winds decrease. Heavy rains fall from the eyewall and from bands of dense clouds that swirl around the eyewall. These bands, called rainbands, can produce more than 5 cm (2 in) of rain per hour. The hurricane draws large amounts of heat and moisture from the sea.

19

WHICH HEMISPHERE DO YOU LIVE IN?

Hemisphere is the name given to any half of the globe. It comes from a Greek word that means half a sphere. Geographers divide the Earth into hemispheres by using the equator as a boundary line. All areas north of the equator make up the northern hemisphere. All areas to the south make up the southern hemisphere. The Earth may also be divided into a land hemisphere and a water hemisphere. The land hemisphere includes the half of the Earth with the most land. Its middle lies near London, England. The other half of the Earth, mostly water, makes up the water hemisphere. Its middle lies near New Zealand.

FACT FILE

The equator is an imaginary line drawn around the outside of the Earth. It divides the Earth into two halves, called hemispheres. It was invented by mapmakers because it makes a convenient point from which to measure distances.

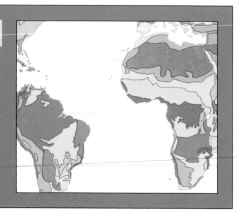

WHICH DAY OF THE YEAR IS THE SHORTEST?

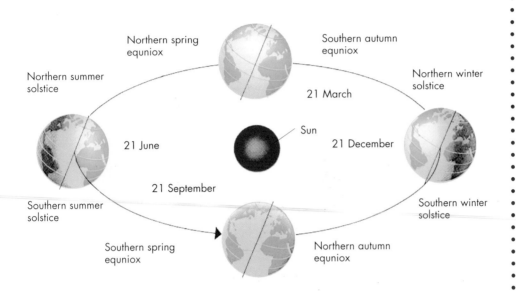

Northern spring equniox

Southern autumn equniox

Northern summer solstice

Northern winter solstice

21 March

21 June

Sun

21 December

21 September

Southern summer solstice

Southern winter solstice

Southern spring equniox

Northern autumn equniox

FACT FILE

Mars is known as the 'Red Planet' because it is covered by a stone desert that contains lots of iron oxide, making it appear rusty red. The water and oxygen that used to exist on Mars are now locked up in these iron deposits; nowadays the planet has hardly any atmosphere.

The shortest day of the year is in the winter solstice which is 21 December. When the northern hemisphere is turned towards the Sun, the countries north of the equator have their summer season, and the countries south of the equator have their winter. When the direct rays of the Sun fall on the southern hemisphere, it is their summer and it is winter in the northern hemisphere. There are two days in the year when night and day are equal all over the world. They come in the spring and fall, just halfway between the two solstices. One is the autumnal equinox in September, and the other is the spring equinox in March.

WHICH PROCESS STARTS THE WATER CYCLE?

Hydrology is the study of the movement and distribution of the waters of the Earth. In nature, water circulates through a system called the water cycle. The process starts with evaporation, when heat from the Sun causes ocean water to vaporize. The vaporized water rises into the atmosphere, where it gradually cools down and forms clouds. The water eventually falls as rain or snow. Most rain and snow falls back into the oceans. But some falls on the land and flows back to the seas, completing the cycle.

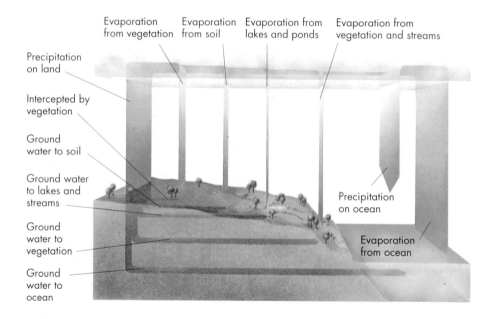

Evaporation from vegetation

Evaporation from soil

Evaporation from lakes and ponds

Evaporation from vegetation and streams

Precipitation on land

Intercepted by vegetation

Ground water to soil

Ground water to lakes and streams

Ground water to vegetation

Ground water to ocean

Precipitation on ocean

Evaporation from ocean

FACT FILE

There are two main sources of fresh water: (1) surface water and (2) ground water. Surface water flows over the land in lakes, rivers, and streams. Ground water seeps through the soil or through tiny cracks in rock.

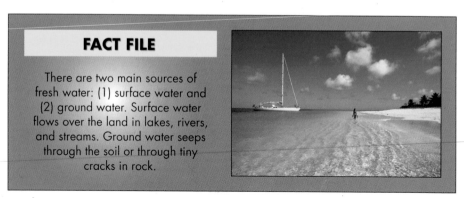

WHICH PROCESS CAUSES ACID RAIN?

Acid rain is a term for rain, snow, sleet, or other wet precipitation that is polluted by such acids as sulphuric acid and nitric acid. It forms when vaporized water in the air reacts with certain chemical compounds. These compounds, including sulphur dioxide and nitrogen oxides, come largely from the burning of coal, gasoline and oil. Most vehicles, factories, and power plants burn such fuels for energy. Acid rain harms thousands of

lakes, rivers and streams worldwide, killing fish and other wildlife. It also damages buildings, bridges and statues. High concentrations of acid rain can harm forests and soil. Regions affected by acid rain include large parts of eastern North America, Scandinavia and central Europe and parts of Asia. Since about the 1950s, the problem has increased in some rural areas. This has occurred because the use of taller smokestacks in urban areas has enabled the winds to transport pollutants further from their original sources.

FACT FILE

Adding lime to lakes and rivers and their drainage areas temporarily neutralizes their acidity. But the neutralization may have harmful side effects.

WHICH AREAS OF THE WORLD ARE MOST SUSCEPTIBLE TO FLOODING?

Flooding occurs when water cannot drain away fast enough in the rivers. In areas of non-porous rocks, water runs off the land very quickly and streams and rivers soon overflow. Flooding also happens when winter snows thaw in spring. Huge floods cover parts of Siberia every spring, when snow melts while the rivers are still iced up. Low-lying coastal lands are vulnerable to flooding, too, especially when gales and high tides cause water to flow inland. Low-lying Bangladesh is particularly liable to this kind of flooding. In addition, melting snow in the Himalayan mountains adds huge amounts of water to Bangladesh's rivers, increasing the flood risk.

FACT FILE

Many of the world's cities are low lying and threatened by flooding. Bangkok, in Thailand, and Venice, in Italy, are typical old cities built by water because they relied on shipping.

WHICH IS EARTH'S LONGEST RIVER?

At 6,650 km (4,132 miles) long, the Nile is Earth's longest river. It travels through eleven African countries on its way to the Mediterranean sea: Tanzania, Uganda, Rwanda, Burundi, the Congo, Kenya, Ethiopia, Eritrea, South Sudan, Sudan and Egypt. Rivers start on the top of hills as small streams channelling the rainfall or as a spring releasing ground water. In the highlands the water can move quickly and has a lot of power. It cuts deep gorges and V-shaped valleys in the softer rocks. The river moves rocks and pebbles along its bed, while lighter sediments are carried or dissolved in the water. When they reach the more gentle slopes, the river becomes wider and moves more slowly. Mud and sand is dropped when the river floods and forms ridges on the river bank. When the river reaches the lower plains it begins to meander.

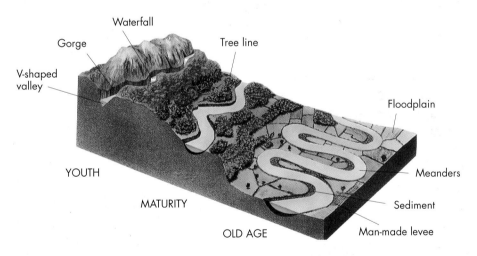

Waterfall

Gorge

Tree line

V-shaped valley

Floodplain

YOUTH

MATURITY

OLD AGE

Meanders

Sediment

Man-made levee

FACT FILE

The further a river is from its source on a mountainside, the slower the water travels. This is because the river eventually reaches flatter ground and widens before it reaches the sea.

WHICH PROCESS CREATES A GLACIER?

Glaciers begin to form when more snow falls during the winter than melts and evaporates in summer. The excess snow gradually builds up in layers. Its increasing weight causes the snow crystals under the surface to become compact, grain-like pellets called firn. At depths of 15 m (50 ft) or more, the firn is further compressed into dense crystals of glacial ice. The ice eventually becomes so thick that it moves, albeit very slowly, under the pressure of its own great weight.

FACT FILE

Glaciers have shaped most of the world's highest mountains, carving out huge valleys. The lakes are formed from flooded glacial valleys that become dammed by debris as the glacier melts.

WHICH PROCESS SHAPES THE COAST?

Coastlines are constantly changing: they are either being eroded or built up and several processes are involved. Waves are very powerful and can remove a large amount of material from a coastline, especially during a storm. The sand and pebbles removed from the coastline are carried by the sea and can be dropped further along a coast or out at sea. Many coastal features, such as sand dunes, spits and salt marshes, can be made by the steady erosion of the cliffs and headlands. A beach can make the waves less powerful and reduce the amount of erosion of the coast. Steep cliffs and wave-cut platforms can be formed in areas of hard rock. A bay can be carved out in an area where hard rock has soft rock between it.

FACT FILE

Many cliffs on the coast are made up of chalk. Chalk is formed from the skeletons of millions and millions of tiny animals called foraminifera. It is a sedimentary rock that formed millions of years ago beneath shallow seas.

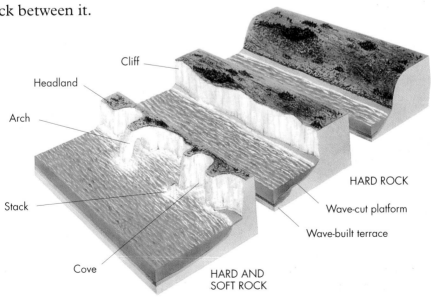

Cliff

Headland

Arch

Stack

Cove

HARD AND
SOFT ROCK

HARD ROCK

Wave-cut platform

Wave-built terrace

WHICH PROCESSES CAUSE EROSION?

Erosion is a natural process by which rock and soil are broken loose from the Earth's surface at one location and moved to another. Erosion changes land by wearing down mountains, filling in valleys and making rivers appear and disappear. It is usually a slow and gradual process that occurs over thousands or millions of years.

Erosion begins with a process called weathering. In this process, environmental factors break rock and soil into smaller pieces and loosen them from the Earth's surface. A chief cause is the formation of ice in colder temperatures. As water freezes, it expands with great force. As a result, when it freezes inside the crack of a rock, it can break the rock apart.

FACT FILE

Erosion can be speeded up by such human activities as farming and mining. One of the most harmful effects of erosion is that it robs farmland of productive topsoil.

WHICH PROCESSES CAUSE DEFORESTATION?

Deforestation is the destruction of the world's rain forest and, sadly, it is down to human activity. In 1950, rain forests covered about 22,533,000 square km (8,700,000 sq miles) of the Earth. This area would cover about three-quarters of Africa. Today, less than half the original extent of the Earth's rain forest remains. In such regions as Madagascar, Sumatra, and the Atlantic coast of Brazil, only small patches still stand. Few rain forest species can adjust to severe disturbance of their habitat. Most perish when people clear large areas of forest. Scientists estimate that tropical deforestation wipes out about 7,500 species per year. Commercial logging, agriculture, mining and hydroelectric dams have all damaged or wiped out extensive areas of rain forest.

FACT FILE

Rain forests benefit people in four major ways. They provide (1) economic, (2) scientific, (3) environmental, and (4) recreational value.

WHICH ROCKS ARE MADE UP OF LAYERS?

The Earth's crust is made up of minerals – substances of a particular chemical combination. Usually minerals form crystals of a particular shape, but sometimes these crystals are distorted or too small to see. When different minerals form together, the result is rock. There are three types of rock sedimentary, igneous and metamorphic. Of these, the sedimentary rocks are formed from fragments that are laid down as layers, or beds.

Sediments pile up in beds on the bottom of a river, or a sea or a lake, or even in a desert, and the weight of the beds on top compress those below. Ground water percolates through the beds, depositing minerals as it goes, and these minerals cement the sedimentary particles together. The result, over millions of years, is a solid mass – a sedimentary rock. In any undisturbed sequence the oldest sedimentary bed is always found at the bottom.

FACT FILE

Sedimentary rocks include the following:

- Conglomerate: this is coarse, like a solidified pebble bed and is formed from shingle beaches.
- Sandstone: medium-grained and formed from sand accumulated in river beds or in deserts.
- Coal: formed as vegetable material piles up in beds and does not rot away.
- Limestone: made from seashells or coral reefs or from dissolved calcite in sea water.

Coal

WHICH ROCKS USUALLY HAVE VISIBLE CRYSTALS?

Of the three main types of rock, igneous rocks are formed when molten material from inside the Earth cools and solidifies. Usually the minerals that make up the rock form distinct crystals. It is quite easy to see the crystals in some igneous rocks. Granite, for example, has big crystals through cooling slowly and is light in colour because of the high proportion of silica in the minerals. It comes from deep in mountain ranges. Gabbro also has big crystals and is dark in colour because of the low proportion of silica in the minerals. It is also found deep in mountain ranges or in the crust of the ocean. Basalt is a very fine-grained rock because of rapid cooling as it is solidified lava flow. It has a black colour because of the low proportion of silica minerals. It comes from freely-flowing volcanoes like the ones on Hawaii or Iceland.

FACT FILE

There are two types of igneous rock. Intrusive rocks are formed under the surface of the Earth and tend to be coarse with big crystals. Extrusive rocks are formed at the surface of the Earth as molten lava from a volcano cools. This is usually fine, with crystals that cannot be seen with the naked eye.

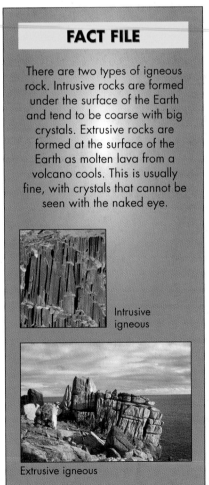

Intrusive igneous

Extrusive igneous

WHICH ROCKS ARE METAMORPHIC?

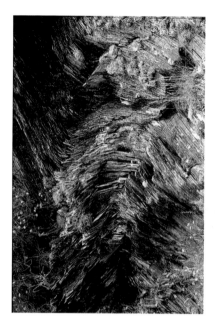

Metamorphic rocks are the result of already existing rocks being heated and compressed by Earth movements to such an extent that their minerals change. The material of the Earth's crust is constantly changing, usually through plate-tectonic activity. Rocks melt and are solidified as igneous rocks. These may break down when exposed and become sedimentary rocks, or may be changed into metamorphic rocks. These then may break down again. With metamorphic rocks, the important thing is that the original rock does not melt – otherwise it would be an igneous rock. There are two types of metamorphic rock, thermal metamorphic (formed principally by the action of heat) and regional metamorphic (formed principally by the action of pressure).

FACT FILE

Examples of metamorphic rock include:

- Marble: forms as limestone is cooked by igneous activity.
- Slate: forms as mountain-building activities act on sedimentary rocks like shale. It splits easily along lines of weakness.
- Schist: forms by more intense mountain-building activities. New minerals are formed along twisted bands.
- Gneiss: forms in the extreme depths of mountains and has big obvious crystals.

WHICH ARE THE MAIN TYPES OF FOSSIL FOUND ON EARTH?

Stages of fossilization: death, decomposition, burial, fossilization.

We know that animals and plants existed long ago on Earth. They have left their remains behind as fossils. For an organism to become a fossil it must be buried rapidly in sediment. This is why we mostly find fossils of animals that live in the water, where sediment is accumulating, and why fossils of land-living animals are very rare. The are four main fossil types:

• The hard parts of living things preserved unaltered, such as sharks' teeth.

• Petrified living things, where the original organic substance is replaced molecule by molecule to produce a fossil with the original structure but made entirely of mineral.

• Casts. When a mould is filled by minerals deposited by ground water, the result is a lump in the shape of the original body, but without the internal structure.

• Trace fossils. Sometimes nothing of the original organism is left – just its burrows or the marks that it made, showing us how it lived but not what it looked like.

FACT FILE

Many of the fossils found on Earth are those of dinosaurs. The fossils help scientists to build a more accurate picture of what these prehistoric creatures might have looked like.

WHICH FOSSIL FUEL ORIGINATED IN THE CARBONIFEROUS PERIOD?

The Carboniferous period took place around 359 to 299 million years ago. By that time, life on the land had become fully established. The period is named after the element carbon, which was abundant at this time. The period came to an end with an ice age that affected most of the southern hemisphere. During the Carboniferous period, newly thrown-up mountain ranges were being quickly eroded and the debris spread out into broad river deltas. These were clothed in thick forests that eventually formed the coal seams of the period. Coal formed from the remains of tree ferns and other primitive trees, which were covered with mud and sand and buried as new rock was laid down. Very gradually, over millions of years, this material turned into coal. A similar process is taking place today in peat bogs, where the rotting remains of heather form peat. When the peat is dried, it burns in a similar way to coal. In some parts of the world a soft shale, called brown coal, is mined. The hardest and most pure form of coal is called anthracite.

FACT FILE

Coal forest plants include club mosses called lepidodendron and sigillaria, calamites, which were horsetails as big as Christmas trees growing as reed beds in shallow water, and cordaites – a primitive relative of the conifers, growing on slightly drier ground. Various ferns formed undergrowth and crept up tree trunks.

WHICH OF EARTH'S PLANTS ARE THE OLDEST?

Ferns are among the oldest kinds of plants that live on land. Scientists believe that ferns appeared on Earth more than 350 million years ago. Ferns differ from flowering plants mainly in the way that they reproduce. They do not have seeds, but reproduce by means of microscopic spores, and they have fronds instead of true leaves. Microscopic spores are produced on the underside of these fronds, and these are scattered by the wind. When the spores land in a suitably damp area, they sprout and grow into a tiny plant that develops small reproductive structures. Sperms fertilize the egg cell, which begins to grow as the tiny plant shrivels and dies, and the complete fern begins to develop.

FACT FILE

Bracken is considered a nuisance in pastures because it is poisonous to livestock. It is hard to get rid of because its rhizome reaches deep underground.

THE NATURAL WORLD

CONTENTS

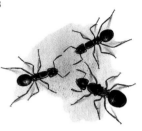

WHICH SYSTEM IS USED FOR NAMING PLANTS AND ANIMALS? 38
WHICH EXPLORER CHAMPIONED THEORIES OF EVOLUTION? 39

WHICH INSECT EATS WOOL? 40
WHICH INSECT HAS ARMIES AMONG ITS SPECIES? 41

WHICH INSECTS MAKE HONEY? 42
WHICH INSECT CAN SING? 43

WHICH INSECTS LIVE IN WATER? 44
WHICH INSECT SPREADS MALARIA? 45

WHICH CREATURES SPIN WEBS? 46
WHICH REPTILES HAVE NO LEGS? 47

WHICH SNAKE FLARES ITS HEAD WHEN ANGRY? 48
WHICH CREATURES ARE HALFWAY BETWEEN FISH AND REPTILES? 49

WHICH ANIMALS ARE VERTEBRATES? 50
WHICH MAMMAL IS THE LARGEST ANIMAL IN THE WORLD? 51

WHICH RHINOS HAVE TWO HORNS? 52
WHICH ANIMAL HAS A FOUR-PART STOMACH? 53

WHICH MAMMALS MIGRATE? 54
WHICH BEARS LIVE AT THE ARCTIC CIRCLE? 55

WHICH CREATURES LIVE IN SETS? 56
WHICH CREATURES ON EARTH ARE UNDER THREAT? 57

WHICH TYPE OF BAT DRINKS BLOOD? 58
WHICH ANIMALS HIBERNATE? 59

WHICH CREATURES MAKE SPAWN? 60
WHICH MALE CREATURES GIVE BIRTH? 61

WHICH BIRD SLEEPS ON ONE LEG? 62
WHICH BIRDS HAVE EYES IN THEIR TAILS? 63

WHICH BIRDS CAN SWIM UNDERWATER? 64
WHICH BIRDS LIVE IN ANTARCTICA? 65

WHICH BIRDS CAN FLY THE FASTEST? 66
WHICH BIRDS MIGRATE THE FURTHEST? 67

WHICH IS THE WORLD'S LARGEST FUNGUS? 68
WHICH PLANT GROUP DO CACTI BELONG TO? 69

WHICH PLANTS HAVE NO TRUE ROOTS? 70
WHICH PLANTS EAT INSECTS? 71

WHICH PART OF A PLANT PRODUCES POLLEN? 72
WHICH IS THE BIGGEST FLOWER OF ALL? 73

ON WHICH TREES DO CONES GROW? 74
WHICH TREE IS THE TALLEST IN THE WORLD? 75

ON WHICH TREE DOES AN ACORN GROW? 76
WHICH TREES ARE EVERGREEN? 77

WHICH PLANTS ARE PERENNIAL? 78
WHICH PLANTS ARE ASSOCIATED WITH CHRISTMAS? 79

WHICH PLANT IS SAID TO BRING GOOD LUCK? 80
WHICH PLANT HELPS YOU SLEEP? 81

WHICH SYSTEM IS USED FOR NAMING PLANTS AND ANIMALS?

It is called the Linnaean system. Most of us know the plants in our gardens and the animals we keep as pets by their common names – daffodil, goldfish, hamster – but these names vary from one language to another. Not only that, but there are so many different types of plants and animals, that a common name like wasp can apply to a number of different insects. In order to avoid confusion, and to allow every plant or animal to be recognized by the same name everywhere in the world, the scientist Carl Linnaeus (1707–1778) came up with a brilliant system using the Latin language. Known as 'binomial nomenclature' or two names, his system uses one word to describe the genus and another to describe the distinguishing characteristic of a specific living thing. At the time of Linnaeus' work Latin, the language of science, was taught everywhere and was uniquely suitable for this system of naming plants and animals.

FACT FILE

The Latin name for a human is Homo sapien, meaning 'thinking man'. A fossil form of Homo, or man, is Homo habillis (tool-using man).

WHICH EXPLORER CHAMPIONED THEORIES OF EVOLUTION?

FACT FILE

We can see how evolution has changed living things by examining fossils. Fossils preserve the body parts of living creatures from long ago so that we can see how they have changed over millions of years.

In the year 1831, the explorer Charles Darwin (1809–1882) set out on an exploratory voyage in the ship *Beagle*, heading for South America. The voyage lasted five years. During this time Darwin kept careful notes of everything he saw. He also collected animal specimens and fossils, which he later turned over to cataloguing expects in Cambridge and London. Darwin was intrigued by what he learned. In South America he had found fossils of extinct armadillos that were similar, but not identical, to the living animals he had seen. This led him to develop his theories on evolution – the idea that animals pass characteristics on from one generation to the next. On 24 November 1859 Darwin published his theories in a book called *On The Origin of Species*. The book caused a great sensation, but it was some time before it was accepted by the scientific world. Eventually it became generally accepted that evolution took place along the lines that Darwin suggested. His theory on evolution of species solved many puzzles.

WHICH INSECT EATS WOOL?

Some people talk of 'clothes moths' making holes in their woollen jumpers and cardigans, and even put mothballs in cupboards and drawers to prevent it happening. While these moths do exist, it is not the moth that does the damage at all. In fact the moth never eats; it lives only to produce its eggs and then it dies. It is when the young moth is in the caterpillar stage that all the damage is done. The moth lays its eggs on woollen fabrics and in about a week the eggs hatch into caterpillars. The caterpillar then makes a little tubular case out of the wool, and lines this case with silk. There it lives as a caterpillar until it is ready to emerge as a moth. So you see that the problem of protecting clothes against moths is to make sure that moths have no chance of laying their eggs on the clothes in the first place.

FACT FILE

When at rest, eyed hawk moths resemble a dead leaf. If alarmed, they open their forewings to reveal striking eye markings on the hind wings. This is likely to scare predators such as birds.

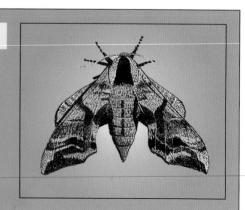

WHICH INSECT HAS ARMIES AMONG ITS SPECIES?

With more than 12,000 species found worldwide, ants live on every continent of the globe, except Antarctica. Of those 12,000 species, around 200 hundred are classed as army ants. These are fierce hunters. Some travel across the land in narrow columns, while others hunt underground, moving through tunnels in the soil. Army ants prey chiefly on other insects and spiders. In some cases, they also kill and eat larger animals that cannot escape quickly.

Most army ant colonies have between 10,000 to several million members. Army ants that live above ground do not build permanent nests. When they rest, they cling together in a large cluster. They may hang from the branch of a tree or roost inside a hollow log or other suitable place. The queen and her brood nest within the large cluster of bodies. Some kinds of army ant hunt for a few weeks and then rest for a few weeks. During the hunting periods, they may nest at a different site every night. During the resting periods, they stay in one place, and the queen lays hundreds or thousands of eggs.

FACT FILE

The black ant has a special relationship with aphids. They collect the sweet honeydew from the aphids and in return protect them from predators such as ladybirds.

WHICH INSECTS MAKE HONEY?

Bees make honey! It is their food. They make it and store it up for the whole bee colony. In order to transport honey nectar home after visiting flowers, the bee has a honey sac, a bag-type growth located in front of the bee's stomach, divided from the stomach by a special valve. It is while the nectar is still in the bee's honey sac that the first stage of making honey occurs, with a chemical change taking place in the nectar's sugar.

Once in the hive, the water is removed from the nectar by evaporation, caused by both ventilation and the heat of the hive. In fact, the honey has so much water removed, it will keep indefinitely when the bee stores it in the honeycombs. The bee puts the honey in the honeycombs to ripen, to be stored as the future food supply for the colony. Bees make different kinds of honey – both in appearance and flavour – depending on the original source of the nectar.

FACT FILE

Honey is removed from the hive by various methods. It may be squeezed from the comb by presses, or it may be sold in the combs cut from the hive. Most honey, however, is removed from the combs by a machine known as 'a honey extractor'.

WHICH INSECT CAN SING?

An insect that is well known for singing is the cricket. These songs are produced primarily by the males. Each kind of cricket has a different song, usually trills or a series of chirps. Crickets produce sound by rubbing their two front wings together. They hear sound with organs in their front legs. Their songs help male and female crickets find each other. Male tree crickets sing in chorus. Their song is a high-pitched treet-treet-treet.

A cricket is a type of jumping insect related to the grasshopper. Crickets differ from grasshoppers in several ways. The wings of most crickets lie flat over each other on top of their backs. Other crickets only have tiny wings or are wingless. The slender antennae are much longer than the body in most kinds of crickets.

Crickets are commonly found in pastures, meadows and along roads. Sometimes they even enter houses. These insects eat plants and the remains of other insects. The best known are the house cricket of Europe and the common cricket of the United States.

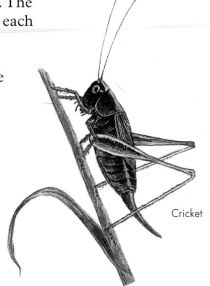
Cricket

FACT FILE

A grasshopper is an insect that can leap about 20 times as far as the length of its body. If a human being had that same leaping ability, he or she could jump about 37 m (120 ft).

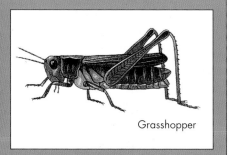
Grasshopper

WHICH INSECTS LIVE IN WATER?

A wide variety of bugs and beetles live in and around water. They can be found in rivers, lakes and ponds – all freshwater habitats. Although they live in or near water, they all breathe air and have to return to the surface of the water from time to time. Ponds and lakes are the best habitats for water bugs. Only a few species of bugs and beetles live in streams and rivers, except in places where the current is slow flowing. Adult water beetles have to breathe air. They do not have gills. Many have a supply of air beneath their wing cases or under the body, which they renew from time to time. Watch a beetle in a tank. Some species come to the surface tail first, while a few come to the surface head first. Count the number of times a beetle will visit the surface in an hour.

FACT FILE

Place a needle on a piece of paper in some water. As the paper sinks, the needle floats, showing surface tension. This same process allows the water boatman to 'walk' on water. It uses its legs like oars to swim.

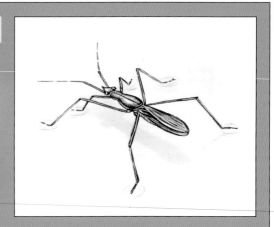

WHICH INSECT SPREADS MALARIA?

A mosquito is an insect that spreads some of the most serious diseases to people and animals. Some mosquitoes carry the germs that cause such deadly diseases as encephalitis, malaria, filariasis and yellow fever.

Mosquitoes do not really bite because they cannot open their jaws. What happens when a mosquito 'bites' is that it stabs through the victim's skin with six needlelike parts called stylets, which form the middle of the mosquito's proboscis. The stylets are covered and protected by the insect's lower lip, which is called the labium.

As the stylets enter the skin, the labium bends and slides upwards out of the way. Then saliva flows into the wound through channels formed by the stylets. The mosquito can easily sip the blood because the saliva keeps it from clotting. Most people are allergic to the saliva, and an itchy welt called a 'mosquito bite' forms on the skin.

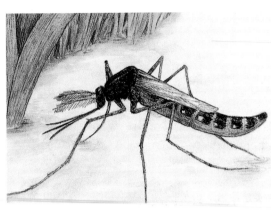

FACT FILE

Only female mosquitoes bite and only the females of a few species attack human beings and animals.

WHICH CREATURES SPIN WEBS?

Everybody knows that spiders spin webs! They spin them from silk, which is pumped out from tiny nozzles, called spinnerets, at the back of the abdomen. As the silk is stretched by the spider into a thread it hardens and becomes proportionately stronger than steel. Some of these threads are quite sticky, while others simply support the web. The spider is able to feel the vibrations of the web when an insect flies into it and it then runs quickly across the web to capture its prey. Usually the insect is wrapped in silk before being eaten by the spider.

FACT FILE

Ants are called arthropods, which means they have a hard outer shell to protect their organs and joints to allow for free movement.

WHICH REPTILES HAVE NO LEGS?

Snakes are reptiles that have no legs. They have several ways of moving about. The most common way is for a snake to throw its body into loops and move forward by pressing against anything solid. Another way in which a snake moves is by contracting its muscles, which pushes the body along rather like a concertina being squeezed open and shut.

The desert-living sidewinder moves by throwing a loop out to one side, then sliding its body towards the loop while throwing another loop sideways at the same time. The sidewinder looks like a spring rolling along the sand, but this is an effective way of moving on this soft surface.

FACT FILE

A reptile is an air-breathing animal with a body structure between that of an amphibian and a mammal. Living reptiles include crocodiles, tortoises and turtles, snakes and lizards.

A sidewinder

WHICH SNAKE FLARES ITS HEAD WHEN ANGRY?

Of all the snakes in the world, it is the cobra that is recognized by the hood that it flares when angry or disturbed. The hood is created by elongated ribs that extend the loose skin of the neck behind the cobra's head. Cobras can be found throughout the Philippines, southern Asia and Africa, and are well known for their intimidating conduct and deadly bite. They are venomous, and their the venom often contains a powerful neurotoxin that acts on the nervous system.

Venoms have some medicinal uses – for example, some are used as painkillers in cases of arthritis or cancer. The king cobra is the world's longest venomous snake. It averages 3.7 m (12 ft) in length but has been known to grow to 5.5 m (18 ft) and has an olive or brown skin, with bronze eyes. The king cobra is found in the Philippines, Malaysia, southern China, Myanmar (formerly known as Burma), India, Thailand and the Malay Peninsula.

FACT FILE

The spotted salamander is one of the larger members of the mole salamander family reaching lengths of nearly 20 cm (8 in) or more.

WHICH CREATURES ARE HALFWAY BETWEEN FISH AND REPTILES?

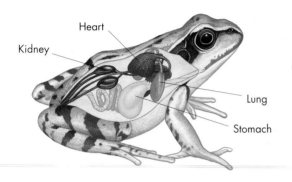

Kidney

Heart

Lung

Stomach

The internal organs of an amphibian

From an evolutionary point of view, amphibians are halfway between fish and reptiles. There are 4,400 living species of amphibian. Frogs, toads, newts and salamanders are all amphibians. Many live mainly on land, but most spend at least some of their lives in water.

Frogs and salamanders are able to breathe through their damp skins to a certain extent, both in the water and on land, but toads must rely largely on their lungs and cannot remain in water for long. Toads and frogs are similar in many ways, although toads usually have rougher, drier skins and may waddle rather than hop as frogs do. Some toad spawn is produced in strings, like necklaces, rather than the mass of eggs laid by a frog. The largest amphibian, the Chinese giant salamander, is 1.8 m (6 ft) long.

FACT FILE

Some brightly coloured amphibians produce poison in glands on their skin. The bright colours warn birds and animals not to eat them. The poisons are among the most powerful known to humans. In South America, poison from the poison arrow frog is added to the arrow tips used by the Indians for hunting.

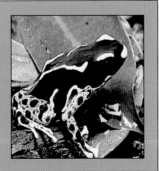

WHICH ANIMALS ARE VERTEBRATES?

An animal is classed as a vertebrate when it has a backbone to provide support for the muscles and protection for the spinal cord. Vertebrates include fish, amphibians, reptiles, birds and mammals. The backbone is actually a series of small bones called vertebrae. They are joined together and locked with rope-like ligaments to provide a flexible but extremely strong anchor for the back muscles. The spinal cord runs down a channel inside the vertebrae, providing protection from damage.

Some primitive fish, such as sharks and rays, have a spine made of a tough rubbery material called cartilage. There are approximately 45,000 living species of vertebrates. In size, they range from minute fishes to elephants and whales (of up to 90 tonnes/100 tons), the largest animals ever to have existed. They are adapted to life underground, on the surface and in the air.

FACT FILE

The duck-billed platypus is a very unusual, small, semi-aquatic mammal. It lives in lakes and streams of eastern Australia and Tasmania. It is notable in having a broad, flat, rubbery snout, webbed feet, and in that it lays eggs.

WHICH MAMMAL IS THE LARGEST ANIMAL IN THE WORLD?

The blue whale is the largest animal that ever lived on Earth. It is also the loudest animal on Earth. These enormous mammals eat tiny organisms, like plankton and krill, which they sift through baleen (a horny substance attached to the upper jaw). They live in pods (small groups). These grey-blue whales have two blowholes and a 5 to 30 cm (2 to 14 in) thick layer of blubber. Blue whales are rorqual whales, that is, whales that have pleated throat grooves that allow their throat to expand during the huge intake of water during filter feeding. Blue whales have 50 to 70 throat grooves that run from the throat to mid-body.

FACT FILE

The largest land mammal is the African elephant, which can weigh up to 7 tonnes (6.9 tons).

WHICH RHINOS HAVE TWO HORNS?

There are five different types of rhinoceros living today, of which two – the black rhinoceros and the white rhinoceros – are found in Africa, and they both have two horns. The other three kinds live in Asia. The Indian and Javan rhinoceroses only have one horn, while the Sumatran rhino has two horns. Rhinoceroses have huge, heavy bodies and usually move about very slowly. They pay little attention to their surroundings and do not hunt other animals for food. Rhinoceroses eat only grass and other plants. The great body of the rhinoceros rests on four short legs. Each foot has three toes. Rhinoceroses are hoofed animals and are related to horses.

FACT FILE

This huge creature is normally very quiet and unassuming. But if it is cornered, it can become very fierce and dangerous. A rhinoceros can charge at a speed of up to 48 km (30 miles) an hour.

WHICH ANIMAL HAS A FOUR-PART STOMACH?

A cow has a stomach with four compartments. This kind of stomach enables a cow to bring swallowed food back into its mouth to be chewed and swallowed again; this is known as chewing the cud. Animals with such stomachs are called ruminants. The compartments are the rumen, the reticulum, the omasum and the abomasum. Each cavity helps digest food with the aid of numerous micro-organisms, such as bacteria and yeasts that live in the stomach. The fourth cavity is the 'true stomach', which functions in the same way as the stomach in human beings and other mammals that are not ruminants.

FACT FILE

Cows, sheep and goats have no front teeth in the upper jaw. Instead, the gums form a tough pad.

WHICH MAMMALS MIGRATE?

FACT FILE

The lemming is a plump little animal related to the mouse. When overcrowding of their habitat and scarcity of food occurs, they are forced to migrate. Every few years, according to legend, great numbers of lemmings march to the sea and drown themselves.

Migrating is when an animal moves from one habitat to another in search of a better climate of a greater abundance of food. Many animals migrate as part of a seasonal cycle, among them elephants, sharks, frogs and many types of bird.

The land animal that travels the furthest when it migrates is the caribou. These live in herds in the cold northern regions and feed on lichen. Each year, when snows bury their food supply, the caribou migrate south to warmer regions – sometimes travelling as far as 1125 km (700 miles) – and return north when the snows thaw. Barren-ground caribou spend the summer in the Arctic tundra and the winter in the evergreen forests south of the tundra. They may be found from western Alaska to western Greenland. In the western part of their range, they live in large herds, and roam for days at a time. They do not overgraze their territory because they keep moving from place to place. In summer, they eat mostly grass and the leaves of various shrubs, while in winter, they live mainly on lichens.

WHICH BEARS LIVE AT THE ARCTIC CIRCLE?

The Arctic region is at the very top of the Earth. The Arctic Circle comprises a shallow, frozen ocean surrounded by the northern edges of Europe, Asia and North America. The area is named after Arktos, the Great Bear star constellation, which dominates the northern polar skies. The Arctic circle area is marked on maps with an imaginary line. Polar bears live here, alongside caribou (reindeer), arctic foxes, seals, whales, narwhals, walruses and sea birds. The polar bear is the world's largest, land-living predator. It spends the winter and spring on the frozen ocean hunting for harp seals and hooded seals. When the ice thaws for the summer, it moves back onto the mainland. The polar bear is one of the world's endangered species and is the only bear with international protection. Each year, as many as 600 polar bears are killed by hunters, who sell their fur for rugs. Scientists estimate there are up to 25,000 polar bears living in the Arctic Circle.

TELL ME WHICH : THE NATURAL WORLD

FACT FILE

The Arctic Ocean is surrounded by icy land. A large section of the ocean is permanently frozen. This is called the ice cap. In the winter, the sea freezes and increases the size of the ice cap so that it touches the land.

WHICH CREATURES LIVE IN SETS?

Badgers are creatures that live in sets. They have distinctive black and white faces, with broad bodies on powerful short legs. They live in colonies, underground – sets – throwing out obvious heaps of soil at the entrances to their tunnels. They emerge from their sets at dusk to forage for food. They prefer hilly districts on the borders of woods or thickets with easily worked soils. They feed on earthworms and other small animals, fruits, cereals and vegetables, using well-worn paths to their chosen pastures or clearings. Badgers take care to keep their sets warm and clean. Damp bedding is thrown out, and fresh, dry grass or straw is scratched up and gathered in armfuls.

FACT FILE

Although foxes and rabbits have earths, badgers usually make the largest and most obvious entrances, with a faint musky scent on their air. You can see their footprints in the soil or snow.

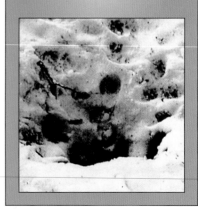

WHICH CREATURES ON EARTH ARE UNDER THREAT?

The ten most endangered species in the world are the tiger, the polar bear, the Pacific walrus, the leatherback turtle, the Magellanic penguin, the bluefin tuna, the monarch butterfly, the mountain gorilla, the Javan rhinoceros and the giant panda.

According to the theory of evolution, some animal species become extinct because they are less successful than other species and are gradually replaced by them. These so-called 'failed' animals are also unable to adapt to changing circumstances. Humans have speeded up their extinction by changing the environment so rapidly that animals do not have the time to adapt. For example, wide-scale destruction of the Indonesian rain forest has left nowhere for the orang-utan to live. It would take millions of years for the animal to evolve into a ground-living creature. Hunting is another reason for the reduced numbers and probable extinction of a number of animals.

FACT FILE

The red wolf became extinct in the wild in 1980, but small numbers of captive specimens were bred. There are now around 200 in captivity.

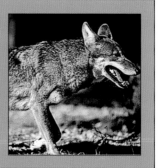

WHICH TYPE OF BAT DRINKS BLOOD?

Vampire bat is the name given to several different bats, particularly to certain bats in Central America and tropical America, which attack horses, cattle, birds and other warm-blooded animals and drink their blood. The best known is the common vampire bat, a small reddish-brown animal about 8 cm (3 in) long. It has very sharp, triangular-shaped front teeth, which cut like a razor. Its oesophagus is short and narrow, and allows

nothing but fluids to pass. Weird stories have been told about the viciousness of these mammals. Their peculiar name comes from the superstitious legends about the vampire, an imaginary being that sucked the blood from human beings.

Many species of bats live in colonies that may have thousands or even millions of members. Others live alone or in small groups. Bats spend the day sleeping in their home, called a roost. They sleep upside down, which enables them to get a speedy take-off when they want to fly away.

FACT FILE

There are many types of bat – among them Whiskered, Geoffrey's, Natterer's and Bechstein's.

Whiskered

Geoffrey's   Natterer's   Bechstein's

WHICH ANIMALS HIBERNATE?

FACT FILE

Many mammals, like the bear, do not really hibernate. They do sleep more in the winter than in the summer, but it is not the deep sleep of hibernation.

The word 'hibernate' comes from the Latin and means 'winter sleep'. Certain animals, including squirrels, hedgehogs, tortoises and bees, hibernate during the winter months to escape the severe weather conditions and because food is hard to find. The sleep of a true hibernator, like the hedgehog, is almost like death and is quite unlike ordinary sleep. The temperature of its body decreases until it is only a little warmer than the air of its den. Because of this, the animal burns the food stored in their bodies very, very slowly. They need less oxygen, and as a result their breathing is slower and their hearts beat only faintly. When spring comes, the animals are awakened by the change in temperature, moisture, and by hunger.

WHICH CREATURES MAKE SPAWN?

Most amphibians lay their eggs in water, and frogs' eggs are called spawn. They are protected from predators by a thick layer of jelly. Inside this a tadpole develops. When it hatches out, it is able to swim, using its long tail, and breathes through gills. As a tadpole grows, first hind legs and then fore legs begin to grow. Lungs develop, and the young frog is able to begin to breathe with its head above water. Gradually the tail shortens until the young frog resembles its adult parents.

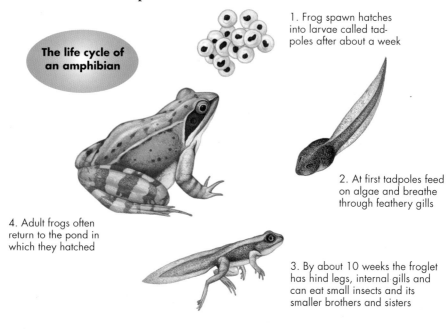

The life cycle of an amphibian

1. Frog spawn hatches into larvae called tad-poles after about a week

2. At first tadpoles feed on algae and breathe through feathery gills

4. Adult frogs often return to the pond in which they hatched

3. By about 10 weeks the froglet has hind legs, internal gills and can eat small insects and its smaller brothers and sisters

FACT FILE

The tree frog lives in the rain forests of South America and uses the pools of water in the centre of certain tropical plants. Although it can swim, it spends much of its life out of water, among the leaves of trees where there are plenty of insects for food. It has sticky toes that enable it to climb.

WHICH MALE CREATURES GIVE BIRTH?

We are accustomed to the idea that it is always the female that bears the offspring, but in seahorses it is the reverse. The seahorse is a small fish that is so named because its head resembles that of a tiny horse. The female seahorse, when she lays her eggs, puts them into the broad pouch beneath the tail of the male. When the young have hatched and are ready to leave the pouch, the mouth of the pouch opens wide. The male alternately bends and straightens his body in convulsive jerks and finally a baby seahorse is shot out. After each birth the male rests, and when all the babies are born he shows signs of extreme exhaustion.

FACT FILE

The seahorse has been described as having the head of a horse, the tail of a monkey, the pouch of a kangaroo, the hard outer skeleton of an insect and the independently moving eyes of a chameleon.

WHICH BIRD SLEEPS ON ONE LEG?

Several wading birds, including herons, cranes and storks, spend time standing on one leg, and some even sleep in that position. Perhaps the best known for doing so is the flamingo, recognized by its stilt-like legs, curved bill, long neck and pink feathers. Flamingos are found in many parts of the world and live near lakes, marshes and seas. They live in colonies, some of which have thousands of members. Flamingos only mate once a year, building a nest that consists of a mound of mud. Most of the females lay a single egg in a shallow hole at the top of the nest, and the parents take turns sitting on the egg to keep it warm.

When they feed, flamingos dip their heads under the water and swing them to and fro, sifting through the water as they walk. The edges of their bills have tiny, narrow crossways plates called lamellae. Their large, fleshy tongues pressing against the inside of the bill strains the water through the lamellae, leaving behind the small invertebrates and the vegetable matter upon which these birds feed.

FACT FILE

Wild flamingos once lived in Florida, but people killed them for their beautiful feathers. The flamingo's feathers vary from bright red to pale pink. For example, flamingos of the Caribbean area have coral-red feathers, and South American flamingos have pinkish-white feathers.

WHICH BIRDS HAVE EYES IN THEIR TAILS?

We often hear the expressions 'as proud as a peacock' or 'vain as a peacock'; this is because the peacock seems to take great pleasure in displaying its beautiful feathers. There are some interesting things about this gorgeous display, which is done solely by the male to attract a female bird. The female, the peahen, does not have these beautiful feathers. The male peacock has a metallic greenish-blue

neck and breast, purplish-blue underparts, and a long train of greenish feathers brilliantly marked with bold spots that look like eyes. These feathers grow from the back and not the tail. During courtship, the male bird spreads the train into a stunning fan as he parades slowly in front of the female. In fact, the male goes through a dance as he tries to convince the peahen that he is a very handsome fellow indeed.

FACT FILE

In ancient times, the peacock was carried to all parts of the world as a great treasure. Both the Greeks and Romans considered it sacred.

WHICH BIRDS CAN SWIM UNDERWATER?

Gannet

Kingfisher

Coot

Birds like the gannet and coot can swim underwater as well as on the surface. Most underwater swimmers, such as cormorants, dive from a floating position on the surface. They give a strong kick, point their heads downwards and dive. Some fish-eating birds, including kingfishers and terns, dive into the water from high in the air. They do not swim but bob to the surface and fly away. Grebes can control the depth at which they swim by regulating the amount of air in their lungs and trapped in their plumage. By slowly letting out some air, they can gradually submerge themselves until only their heads show above the surface, like a periscope, thus they can swim along unnoticed and watch for enemies at the same time.

FACT FILE

The spoonbill is a long-legged wading bird that has a spoon-shaped bill. The bird swings its bill from side to side in the water to search for food.

WHICH BIRDS LIVE IN ANTARCTICA?

Antarctica is a mountainous continent that is almost completely covered by a gigantic sheet of ice larger than Europe and the United States put together. It is the coldest and windiest place on Earth. Average winter temperatures reach –60°C (–76°F), and roaring, ferocious winds of up to 290 km (180 miles) per hour produce blizzards and snowdrifts. The Antarctic has very little ice-free land, even in summer. Blue whales, orcas and fur seals live in the ocean, but there are very few plants and animals on land. One creature that thrives here is the penguin. Several species inhabit and breed in the region, including Adelie, rockhopper and emperor penguins, king penguins, chinstraps and gentoo penguins. Emperor penguins are the largest and grow to around 1 m (40 in) tall.

FACT FILE

The name Antarctica means 'opposite the Arctic'. When it is summer in the Arctic it is winter in Antarctica. More than 90% of all the world's fresh water is stored in the ice sheets on Antarctica, and on Greenland in the Arctic region.

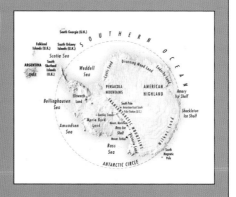

WHICH BIRDS CAN FLY THE FASTEST?

It is easy to assess the speed of horses and people in races because there is a start and a finish line, but it is much harder to measure the speed of a bird in flight. Many figures have been published about the speed in flight of various birds but most authorities

doubt these statistics. In general, the heavier the bird is, the faster it fly in order to stay in the air. One expert believes that the fastest recorded flight for a bird was that of a homing pigeon going at 151.6 km (94.2 miles) per hour.

Here are the estimated speeds that some birds fly at. The peregrine falcon can fly at about 105–120 km (65–75 miles) per hour and the next fastest are ducks and geese who can go at about 105–112 km (65–70 miles) per hour. The European swift, golden plover and dove can reach 95–105 km (60–65 miles) per hour, while hummingbirds reach speeds of 88–95 km (55–60 miles) an hour. Starlings fly at about 72–80 km (45–50 miles) and swallows usually at about 32 km (25 miles) per hour.

FACT FILE

Some birds cannot fly at all. Such birds include penguins who use their wings in water, enabling them to swim very fast. The penguin shown to the right is a rare yellow-eyed species. There are only about 3,000 of them left in the world.

WHICH BIRDS MIGRATE THE FURTHEST?

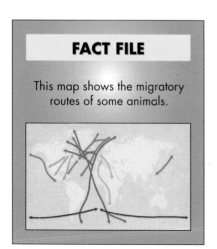

Now we know why birds migrate, the next question is how far do they actually fly to find better conditions. The champion among birds that migrate is the Arctic tern. This amazing bird will travel as many as 35,000 km (22,000 miles) during the course of a year, going back and forth. It nests over a wide range from the Arctic Circle to as far south as Massachusetts. It will take this bird about 20 weeks to make its trip down to the Antarctic region and it averages about 1,600 km (1,000 miles) a week. Most land birds only make short journeys during their migrations. But there is one bird, the American golden plover, that makes a long nonstop flight over the open ocean. It may fly from Nova Scotia directly to South America, a distance of about 3,800 km (2,400 miles), without even stopping. We are not certain that birds start and end their migrations on exactly the same day each year. But there is one bird who comes pretty close to it. The famous swallows of Capistrano, California, are thought to leave on 23 October and return on 19 March, although there is some variation.

FACT FILE

This map shows the migratory routes of some animals.

WHICH IS THE WORLD'S LARGEST FUNGUS?

The giant puffball is the largest known fungi in the world. These puffballs are ball-shaped fungi, and may be any shade from white to tan. They range in size from smaller than a golf ball to larger than a basketball. It can grow as large as 150 cm (60 in), although an average fruit body of a puffball is the size of a football. Just one fruit body will produce about 7,000,000,000,000 spores. When a puffball matures, its spores become dry and powdery. If touched, the puffball breaks open and the spores escape in a smoke-like puff.

Black bovista

Scaly meadow puffball

FACT FILE

Flies and other insects are attracted to the stinking, slimy spore mass of the common stinkhorn. When they fly off after feeding, they carry away spores stuck on to their bodies. This is the way in which the common stinkhorn spreads to new locations.

WHICH PLANT GROUP DO CACTI BELONG TO?

FACT FILE

Cacti have many rare and beautiful features, developed during a long and slow evolutionary process. One of their principal characteristics is the ability to adapt to harsh conditions that would cause most other plant groups to perish quickly.

Cacti get their name from the Greek word *kaktos* meaning thistle and they belong to the succulents group of plants. Succulents are plants that have leaves, stems or roots that can store water so that they can survive extended periods of drought. All the plants in the cactus family are considered stem succulents. During periods of moisture, their stems swell and then during droughts they slowly contract. Cacti with ribs are particularly well adapted to surviving droughts as their ribs expand and contract like an accordion.

69

WHICH PLANTS HAVE NO TRUE ROOTS?

Liverworts, hornworts and mosses do not have true roots. Instead, they are anchored to the ground by hair-like structures called rhizoids that resemble roots. A liverwort absorbs water over its entire surface and dries out quickly. Consequently, liverworts grow extremely close to the ground and often measure less than 1.4 cm (½in) high. Most liverworts grow only in damp, shady environments, such as rotten logs, stream banks and moist cliffs.

Moss has a short stem, which grows from the rhizoids. It is covered by tiny leaves in a spiral pattern. The leaves contain chlorophyll, a green substance that the plant uses to make food. In many cases, a vein runs the length of the leaf from the stem to the tip. This vein, called the costa or midrib, strengthens the leaf and transports food and water. Many mosses grow in moist or aquatic environments. However, some can survive in very dry conditions. Their need for water changes with the amount of water available.

FACT FILE

Lichens have no roots. They have an outer layer of fungal cells that are pigmented green, brown or yellow. This protective layer, called the upper cortex, covers a zone of green or blue-green algal cells.

WHICH PLANTS EAT INSECTS?

Plants growing in bogs and peaty areas often need to supplement their food supply by catching insects. Bog water contains very little nitrogen, but some bog plants can obtain this substance by catching and digesting insects. They are known as insectivorous plants. Other insectivorous plants are covered with sticky tentacles that trap flies. The most remarkable is the Venus flytrap plant. It has two clawed plates that slam together when a fly walks over them and touches a trigger hair. Other insect-eating plants are aquatic, catching tiny crustaceans in bladder-shaped underwater traps. Some of the largest insectivorous plants live in tropical rain forests.

FACT FILE

Some insects use camouflage to blend into their environment, protecting themselves from predators.

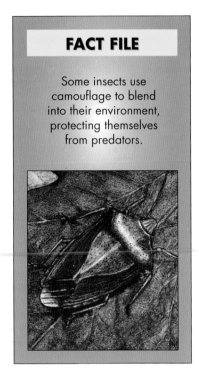

Venus flytrap

WHICH PART OF A PLANT PRODUCES POLLEN?

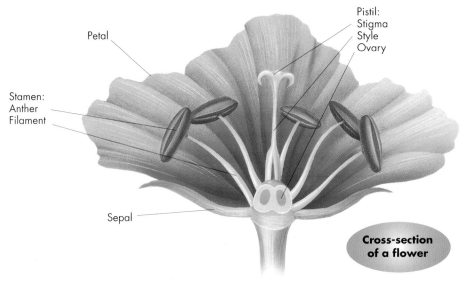

Petal

Pistil:
Stigma
Style
Ovary

Stamen:
Anther
Filament

Sepal

**Cross-section
of a flower**

Pollen grains are produced by the stamens, the male organs of a flower. A flower has four main parts. There is a green outer cup made up of leaf-like sepals. Within the sepals are the petals. Within the petals are the reproductive organs necessary for producing seeds. In the middle are one or more pistils. Around the pistils is a ring of stamens. The pistil is the female part of the flower. The bottom of this is enlarged and it is called the ovary. Inside the ovary are little round ovules which later form into seeds. But they can only become seeds if they are fertilized by the contents of a pollen grain. The pollen must go through the top of the pistil and reach the ovules at the bottom. This fuses with the egg cell and completes the process of fertilization. Pollen can also be carried by the wind or by insects feeding on the nectar.

FACT FILE

Pollen is the plant's equivalent of an animal's sperms. It carries the male reproductive genes. Pollen grains have a pattern, allowing the plant to be identified.

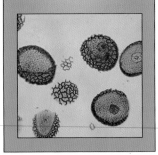

WHICH IS THE BIGGEST FLOWER OF ALL?

The biggest flower of all is called the rafflesia, a parasitic plant that does not photosynthesize. It grows in the rain forests of southeast Asia. The plant actually grows underground and is not visible until a huge bud appears, somewhat like a cabbage. This opens up into a leathery flower which is approximately 1 m (3 ft) across and weighs up to 10 kg (22 lb). The flower is not pretty, it looks and smells just like a huge lump of rotting flesh. It attracts thousands of flies, which pollinate the flower as they walk on it.

FACT FILE

Green algae are the smallest plants. They form, for example, a greenish film often found on the bark of trees. Millions of cells of algae are needed to cover the tree trunk.

ON WHICH TREES DO CONES GROW?

Cones grow on pine trees, which grow cones in order to reproduce. The pine cone is actually a highly modified branch which takes the place of a flower. Separate male cones and female seed cones are borne on the same tree. Each of the numerous scales of the male cone bears pollen, while each female cone scale bears ovules in which egg cells are produced. In the pine the male cones are small and short-lived, and are borne in clusters at the top of the tree. At the time of pollination, enormous numbers of pollen grains are released and dispersed by the wind. Those that land accidentally on female cone scales extend pollen tubes part way into the ovule during one growing season but usually do not reach the stage of actual fertilization until the next year. The cones that are usually seen are the seed cones, which are normally hard and woody.

FACT FILE

Scots pine trees need to be tough to survive long, cold winters. They have thousands of tiny, needle-like leaves, which have a waterproof coating to protect them from the rain and snow.

WHICH TREE IS THE TALLEST IN THE WORLD?

Californian giant redwoods are some of the oldest and largest living organisms on Earth. They often exceed 90 m (300 ft) in height, and their trunks reach typical diameters of 3 to 6 m (10 to 20 ft). The redwood tree takes 400 to 500 years to reach maturity, and some trees are known to be more than 1,500 years old. These ancient trees have very few branches and leaves, and are often scarred by fire and lightning strikes. As the tree ages, the lower limbs fall away, leaving a clear, columnar trunk. The oldest-known trees are bristlecone pine trees. They grow in the White Mountains in California, in the United States. Although they are quite small, some of these gnarled trees are more than 4,500 years old.

FACT FILE

Trees manufacture their own food through a process called photosynthesis. The leaves use carbon dioxide and sunshine to make sugar, starches and cellulose, which are then used to make new cells.

ON WHICH TREE DOES AN ACORN GROW?

The acorn is the fruit of the oak tree. In the spring, oaks produce small, yellowish-green flowers. The male flowers, which form in dangling clusters called catkins, produce large amounts of pollen. The wind carries the pollen to the female flowers and fertilizes them. Once fertilized, a female flower will become an acorn. Acorns vary in length from less than 13 mm (½ in) to more than 5 cm (2 in). Oaks grow slowly and usually do not bear acorns until they are about 20 years old. Most oaks live for 200 to 400 years.

FACT FILE

The oak leaf roller moth lays small groups of eggs on oak twigs. In spring, the caterpillar feeds on oak leaves, which they roll up with silk.

WHICH TREES ARE EVERGREEN?

Certain trees, like pines and firs, are called evergreens. They have narrow, needlelike leaves with a thick, waxy outer covering which prevents the evaporation of water. Consequently the leaves on such trees remain for several years. When the leaves do fall, new ones grow at the same time and the branches never look bare. That is why these types of trees are called evergreens.

On deciduous trees, leaves have several functions and one of them is to make food. Leaves take in carbon dioxide from the air and water and minerals from the soil. The chlorophyll in the leaves absorbs energy from the sun. Sunshine forces the chlorophyll to change the carbon dioxide and water into sugar. The sugar made in the leaves is the tree's basic foods. Leaves also give off enormous quantities of water.

FACT FILE

Fertilizers are used to make crops grow larger and faster. Crops are also regularly sprayed with pesticides and herbicides. There are fears that the chemicals could cause health problems.

Norway Spruce

Corsican Pine

WHICH PLANTS ARE PERENNIAL?

Perennial plants are those that survive from one year to the next, like daffodils and orchids. They usually grow quite slowly, and can afford to build up their strength before they need to produce seeds. The parts of perennial plants that are above the ground are generally killed by frost in the autumn, but the roots and/or underground parts live through the winter. Growth is renewed and the cycle begins anew in the spring.

Perennial plants that grow in arid or desert conditions commonly survive dry times by becoming physiologically inactive. In some cases they remain alive but are dehydrated until water becomes available, at which time they rapidly absorb moisture through above ground parts, swelling and resuming physiological activity. Some plants can absorb dew, which for many is the main water source. Mosses and lichens adopt this strategy, as do some flowering plants, which are sometimes called resurrection plants.

FACT FILE

As well as looking very like small bees, the flowers of bee orchids actually produce a female bee 'smell'. They are therefore highly attractive to male bees.

Early purple orchid

Daffodil

WHICH PLANTS ARE ASSOCIATED WITH CHRISTMAS?

Holly has been used traditionally in houses and churches at Christmastime for decorative purposes. It was originally called the holy tree. The word holly may have come from this name. Holly is the common name for a group of shrubs and small trees. The two best-known hollies, the American holly and the English holly, are evergreens. These two hollies have glossy green leaves and red berries and are used to make attractive Christmas wreaths. Holly wood is very hard and has a close grain. It is used for making musical instruments, furniture and in interior decoration. The inner bark yields the sticky material called birdlime. The leaves of a South American species are used to make a tea-like drink called mate.

FACT FILE

The poinsettia is a popular houseplant also used as a Christmas decoration. What look like the bright red petals are actually a kind of leaf. The real flowers are the tiny green dots in the middle.

WHICH PLANT IS SAID TO BRING GOOD LUCK?

Clover is said to bring luck, but only when it has four leaves. This is because clover is known for its three-lobed (or trifoliate) leaves. The lucky 'four-leaved clover' can be found, but it is an abnormal rarity. Clovers are members of the pea family. There are around 250 kinds of true clovers, including the red, white, strawberry and crimson species. Clovers are generally grassland plants and they are most common near the coast and on chalky or clay soils. Red clover has been used for centuries as a rotation crop. Today, it is used extensively as an animal food and soil-improving crop throughout Europe and northern and central North America.

FACT FILE

Clover flowers are very rich in nectar and so attract many insects. The white base of the flower has a lovely taste, a bit like fresh honey.

WHICH PLANT HELPS YOU SLEEP?

It is said that placing a lavender bag under the pillow at night will help you to sleep, because of the oils in its flowers. Lavender comes from a Latin word that means to wash. This name may have been used because the ancient Romans used the leaves and flowers of the plant to scent their bathwater. In the past, women used to keep dried lavender flowers with their linen and clothing. Today, the dried flowers are used in fragrant sachets and potpourri mixtures. The flowers are also distilled to make an oil that is used in some perfumes.

Lavender has long, narrow, pale green leaves and pale purple flowers. This shade of purple is called lavender after the flowers. The flowers grow in clusters around the stem. When dried, they keep their fragrance for a long time.

FACT FILE

The petals of certain flowers contain sweet-smelling oils. Such flowers include jasmines, mimosas and roses. The oils obtained from the petals of these flowers supply the fragrances for many high-quality perfumes.

HISTORY

CONTENTS

WHICH EVENT RESULTED IN THE GREAT EXTINCTION?   84
WHICH WAS THE WORLD'S FIRST GREAT CIVILIZATION?   85

WHICH ANCIENT CIVILIZATION USED HIEROGLYPHICS?   86
IN WHICH COUNTRY WAS ANCIENT CARTHAGE?   87

WHICH DYNASTY WAS THE FIRST TO RULE CHINA?   88
WHICH KING ORDERED THE DOMESDAY BOOK?   89

WHICH EPIDEMIC CHANGED THE FACE OF MEDIEVAL EUROPE?   90
WHICH CITY IS MOST ASSOCIATED WITH THE RENAISSANCE?   91

WHICH REGIONS WERE CONNECTED BY THE SILK ROAD?   92
WHICH CONTINENT WAS KNOWN AS THE NEW WORLD?   93

WHICH NATION'S FLAG IS THE STAR-SPANGLED BANNER?   94
WHICH EVENT SPARKED THE FRENCH REVOLUTION?   95

WHICH PUBLICATION PIONEERED WOMEN'S RIGHTS?   96
WHICH CANAL WAS BUILT TO LINK THE MEDITERRANEAN
WITH THE RED SEA?   97

WHICH EMPEROR MODERNIZED JAPAN?   98
WHICH WAS AMERICA'S FIRST NATIONAL PARK?   99

WHICH COUNTRY LED THE INDUSTRIAL REVOLUTION?   100
IN WHICH CITY WOULD YOU FIND BIG BEN?   101

IN WHICH CITY WOULD YOU FIND LIBERTY ISLAND?   102
WHICH EVENT LED TO THE EASTER RISING?   103

WHICH EVENT TRIGGERED WORLD WAR I?   104
WHICH MACHINES MADE THEIR DEBUT IN
WORLD WAR I?   105

WHICH FOUR WORLD LEADERS SIGNED THE
TREATY OF VERSAILLES?   106
WHICH EVENT TRIGGERED WORLD WAR II?   107

WHICH EVENT ENDED WORLD WAR II?   108
WHICH PRESIDENT LED THE UNITED STATES OUT
OF THE GREAT DEPRESSION?   109

WHICH EVENT SPARKED THE CUBAN MISSILE CRISIS?   110
WHICH ASSOCIATION HELPS TO KEEP THE PEACE?   111

WHICH EVENT RESULTED IN THE GREAT EXTINCTION?

At the end of the Cretaceous period there was a great extinction of dinosaurs. Although no one knows exactly what caused this great extinction, many scientists believe that the Earth was hit by a meteorite or comet 65 million years ago. Something like this could have caused shock waves that would have killed everything in its vicinity and seismic sea waves (tsunamis)

FACT FILE

Another theory is that changing climates were behind the great extinction. The end of the Cretaceous period shows signs of increasing temperatures. The dinosaurs and the other big animals may have become so well adapted to the equable climates of the Mesozoic era that they did not have the capability to cope with any dramatic change.

that would have flooded all the lowlands. Clouds of dust would have cut off the sunshine, causing short-term global cooling, and would have produced a long-term greenhouse effect.

A buried structure looking like a meteorite crater of the right size and age has been found in Yucatán in Mexico, which would support this theory. Other examples of geological evidence include sedimentary rocks discovered in Texas that look like tsunami deposits, and deposits of quartz crystals that show signs of being deformed by a heavy impact.

WHICH WAS THE WORLD'S FIRST GREAT CIVILIZATION?

The Indus Valley civilization was one of the world's first great societies. It developed out of farming and herding communities that carried on trade with each other. The civilization began to flourish about 4,500 years ago and was based in the vast river plains of what are now Pakistan and northwestern India. There were two main cities – Harappa in the north of the Indus Valley and Mohenjo Daro in the south. They were both carefully planned cities and laid out on a grid system. They had wide roads and brick houses, most of which had at least two storeys. Most homes had a bathing area that was supplied with water from a nearby public well or from a well in the courtyard of the house. The people who lived there were farmers, tending to fields and watering crops with silt-laden waters washed down when the snows melted in the mountains to the north.

FACT FILE

The farmers of the Indus Valley used wooden carts pulled by a pair of oxen. Deep grooves made by heavily laden carts have been found in the excavated streets of Mohenjo Daro.

WHICH ANCIENT CIVILIZATION USED HIEROGLYPHICS?

Egyptian picture writing is known as hieroglyphics. This language is made up of about 750 signs, with pictures of people, animals and objects. Until hieroglyphics was deciphered in modern times, it was not known that most of the pictures represented sounds and syllables, not whole words. Scribes used a quick form of writing, which was called hieratic.

The ancient Egyptians lived in the Nile area of north Africa in around 3000 BCE. They were good at maths, particularly geometry, which they used in architecture – particularly for their temples and pyramids – and surveying. They drew up an accurate 12-month calendar of 365 days, and used water clocks to measure time.

FACT FILE

The Egyptian Sun god Ra was often portrayed in picture form simply as a Sun disk. He appeared in other forms too, including a cat, a bird and a lion.

Chest from tomb of Tutankhamen

IN WHICH COUNTRY WAS ANCIENT CARTHAGE?

Carthage was on the Mediterannean coast of what is now Tunisia, on the eastern side of Lake Tunis. According to legend, it was founded by Queen Dido in 814 BCE as an outpost of the Phoenician Empire, which was based in Tyre (now in southern Lebanon). Over the following centuries it became dominant in the western Mediterannean but as the Roman Empire grew in strength, conflict became inevitable and Rome won all the three wars between them. In the first Punic War, Rome gained Sicily, then later annexed Sardinia and Corsica. In the second, Hannibal failed to regain territory while in the third, Rome destroyed the city of Carthage and took over the Carthaginian empire.

FACT FILE

Thynes, a settlement on the site of present-day Tunis, was part of the ancient empire of Carthage. The settlement gradually developed into the city of Tunis.

WHICH DYNASTY WAS THE FIRST TO RULE CHINA?

The Shang dynasty was the earliest known Chinese ruling family. The dynasty governed from about 1766 BCE to about 1122 BCE. Its centre was in what is now known as the northern Henan Province. Shang society, though based on agriculture, became famous for its fine carvings and bronze work. Most Shang relics found by archaeologists come from Anyang, a city with houses, palaces, temples and elaborate tombs. The people of the Shang period used bronze to make vessels, weapons and chariot fixtures. They also carved marble and jade and wove silk. The Shang kings were superstitious and consulted 'oracle bones' before making any important decisions.

Shang food vessel

FACT FILE

The Shang writing system had more than 3,000 symbols. It appears on pieces of bone, silk and even turtle shells.

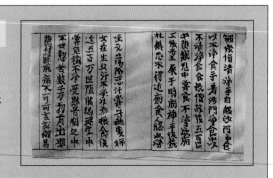

WHICH KING ORDERED THE DOMESDAY BOOK?

At the Battle of Hastings in 1066, William the Conqueror of France fought the Saxon King Harold for the crown of England. William won and was king. Once the Normans had secured their hold over their new territory, they wanted to know exactly what it was worth. In 1085 William I ordered a survey of land in England. The findings were written down in the Domesday Book (Domesday means 'Day of Judgement'). It is the best record we have of life in England between 1066 and 1088, naming about 13,000 towns and villages. This book listed every single town, village, farm, who owned what and how much each holding was worth, so that taxes could be applied. This book is still in existence today.

FACT FILE

Conwy castle, in north Wales, is typical of the castles built by the Normans. It was built to give defending archers an uninterrupted field of fire against any attackers, and could withstand a long siege.

WHICH EPIDEMIC CHANGED THE FACE OF MEDIEVAL EUROPE?

The bubonic plague (or 'Black Death') was a deadly disease, which brought death to most parts of Asia, North Africa and Europe. The first outbreak was recorded in 1331 in China. It probably arrived in Europe from Central Asia by way of Mongol raiders. It first caused epidemics in Italy in 1347, spreading rapidly through the rest of Europe.

Infected houses were marked with an 'X'.

The plague started as a bloody swelling in the armpit or groin and quickly invaded the whole body. It was highly contagious and killed millions of people. The infection probably began on the steppes, the grassy plains of Asia. It was carried by fleas, which lived in the fur of the black rat. The rats lived close to humans and thus the disease spread rapidly. Corpses were left out in the road for people to collect thus spreading the disease further.

FACT FILE

Medieval paintings often depicted death as a skeleton, dancing and leading victims to their end. The epidemic killed at least 25 million people in Europe and the Near East.

WHICH CITY IS MOST ASSOCIATED WITH THE RENAISSANCE?

Florence, in Italy, is the city most associated with the Renaissance. Meaning 'rebirth' the Renaissance was a 14th- to 17th-century period of political, artistic, scientific, cultural, literary and social rebirth, especially in classical studies like mathematics, architecture and philosophy.

The movement spread from Florence throughout Italy and then into western Europe. It is thought that the patronage of wealthy and powerful families like the Medici in Florence, and the arrival of scholars and classical texts from Greece, following the collapse of the Ottoman Empire may have been catalysts for this wide-reaching creativity.

FACT FILE

A column designed by Andrea Palladio, one of the great Renaissance architects. His buildings were designed using classical ideas.

WHICH REGIONS WERE CONNECTED BY THE SILK ROAD?

The Silk Road was a group of ancient trade routes that connected China and Europe. The Silk Road flourished primarily from 100 BCE to 1500 CE. The routes stretched across about 8,050 km (5,000 miles) of mountains and deserts in central Asia and the Middle East between eastern China and the Mediterranean Sea. The Silk Road got its name from the vast amount of Chinese silk carried along it. The cities along the Silk Road provided food, water and rest, as well as goods for trade. Of these cities, Khotan (now Hotan, China) was famous for its jade. The region of Fergana in present-day Uzbekistan was known for its powerful horses.

Camel caravans carried most goods across the dry, harsh regions along the Silk Road. By 800 CE, traffic began to decrease as traders started to travel by safer sea routes. A final period of heavy use occurred during the 13th and 14th centuries, when the Mongols ruled Central Asia and China.

FACT FILE

The Chinese were the first to learn to make silk, and they guarded their secret closely. China was the only supplier of silk until the 6th century CE, when Western countries discovered how to make the fabric.

WHICH CONTINENT WAS KNOWN AS THE NEW WORLD?

European explorers sailed across the Atlantic to what they called the New World of North, Central and South America. There they discovered a treasure trove of gold and silver. They also discovered foods that only grew in the New World, such as sweetcorn, potatoes and plants that could be made into medicines. The people that settled in the New World were traders rather than soldiers. Their first contact with the people already living there was friendly. The Native Americans showed the newcomers how to hunt, fish and farm in a land of plenty. In return they were given objects such as knives, needles, fish hooks and cloth.

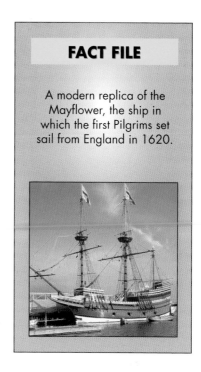

FACT FILE

A modern replica of the Mayflower, the ship in which the first Pilgrims set sail from England in 1620.

By 1550, Spain ruled most of Central and South America and the West Indies. Fleets of Spanish galleons carried gold, silver and plundered treasures across the Atlantic to Europe.

WHICH NATION'S FLAG IS THE STAR-SPANGLED BANNER?

The 'Star-spangled Banner', also known as the Stars and Stripes and 'Old Glory', is the flag of the United States of America. It consists of white stars (50 from July 4, 1960) on a blue background, with a field of 13 alternate stripes, 7 red and 6 white. The 50 stars stand for the 50 states of the Union, and the 13 stripes stand for the original 13 states that signed the Declaration of Independence. After the beginning of the American Revolution, the first unofficial national flag – known variously as the Grand Union Flag, the Great Union Flag, or the Cambridge Flag – was hoisted outside Boston, on 1 January 1776. It was hoisted at the behest of General George Washington, whose headquarters were nearby. The flag had seven red and six white horizontal stripes and, in the background, the British Union Flag (the immediate predecessor of the Union Jack).

FACT FILE

In 1775 George Washington was elected as commander-in-chief of the colonists' army. He became a leading symbol for independence.

WHICH EVENT SPARKED THE FRENCH REVOLUTION?

On 14 July 1789, a mob attacked the royal prison in Paris, the Bastille. Although only a few prisoners were released, this event marked the end of royal power in France and the beginning of the revolution. During the 1700s France was not prosperous. The government was short of money and needed to raise taxes. Louis XVI could only do this by recalling a traditional assembly, which promptly demanded political reforms. He responded by trying to dismiss the assembly, but the citizens in Paris revolted in support of the assembly. The new National Assembly showed its strength by introducing fresh laws in 1791, insisting on freedom and equality. The royal family was imprisoned for a while, then tried and executed.

FACT FILE

Napoleon was a very effective military leader and politician. He ruled France for 15 years, expanding their empire abroad.

WHICH PUBLICATION PIONEERED WOMEN'S RIGHTS?

The women's rights movement had its roots in the late 1700s and early 1800s. Changes such as the American and French revolutions promoted ideas of 'equality' and 'liberty', yet women were not permitted to vote, and most had limited access to education. In 1792, a British writer called Mary Wollstonecraft published *A Vindication of the Rights of Women*, setting out her belief in equal rights for men and women. This idea took a firm hold during the 1800s, and many women started to campaign for reform. The suffragettes engaged in many different forms of protest, including chaining themselves to railings outside the residence of the British Prime Minister.

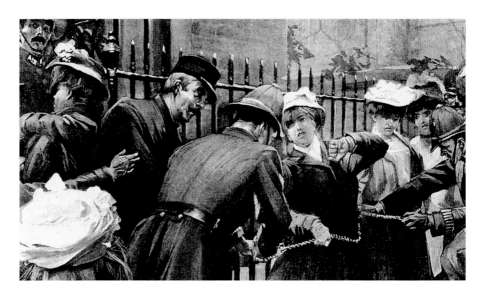

FACT FILE

In Britain, the suffragette campaigners often went on hunger strike when imprisoned for their actions. The authorities did not want them to die, and arouse public sympathy, so they fed the women by force.

WHICH CANAL WAS BUILT TO LINK THE MEDITERRANEAN WITH THE RED SEA?

The idea of a canal linking the Mediterranean to the Red Sea dates back to ancient times. It was Napoleon's engineers who, around 1800, revived the idea of a shorter route to India via the Suez Canal. It was not until 1859 that Egyptian workers started working on the construction of the Canal in conditions, described by historians, as slave labour. The project was completed around 1867. Although Britain had played no part in building the Suez Canal in Egypt, it benefited greatly when it opened. The new 190 km (118 mile) waterway shortened the route from Britain to India by around 9,700 km (6,000 miles), thereby extending their powers of trading.

FACT FILE

Queen Victoria was on the throne when the Suez Canal was first started and when it opened. During her reign, which lasted 63 years, Britain's empire expanded greatly.

WHICH EMPEROR MODERNIZED JAPAN?

Japan embarked on a programme of modernization under Emperor's Mutsuhito in the 1870s. The 1860s had been a time of uncertainty and political unrest in Japan. Finally, in 1868, the situation became so serious that Emperor Mutsuhito took control from the last shogun. Mutsuhito became known as the Meiji emperor, and this event is called the 'Meiji restoration'. In 1872, a group of Japanese politicians went on a tour of Europe and North America to learn more about industry, education and ways of life in the West. As a result, factories were built in Japan and the country started to change from an agricultural to an industrialized nation. This also included the establishment of a national railway system. During the period of Meiji rule, education was introduced for all Japanese people. The Meiji emperor also gave farmers ownership of their lands and changed Japan's army and navy into modern military forces.

FACT FILE

During the Meiji period, Japan wanted to extend its territories. In 1894–1895 its forces crushed the Chinese navy and gained control of Taiwan. Here you can see a Chinese ship sinking during the Battle of Yalu in 1894.

WHICH WAS AMERICA'S FIRST NATIONAL PARK?

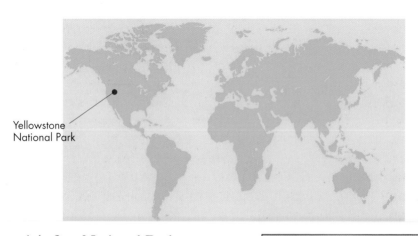

Yellowstone National Park

Amercia's first National Park was Yellowstone National Park, established in 1872. It covers parts of Wyoming, Montana and Idaho. It is famous for its geothermal springs and geysers, such as the spectacular Old Faithful. These geysers result from continuing volcanic activity under the area. The whole area is sitting over a series of calderas caused by a supervolcano (the caldera is the crater left after a massive eruption in which the magma chamber is emptied rapidly and the ground above collapses into it).

The supervolcano under Yellowstone is the result of a 'hotspot', a plume of molten lava rising from deep within the earth. About 2.2 million years ago, a massive explosion blew 2,500 km^3 (600 miles^3) of material into the air covering most of North America in ash. The park's stunning landscape is home to bison, bears, elk, American bald eagles and trumpeter swans.

FACT FILE

Old Faithful is a relatively predictable geyser, whose eruptions occur between 55 and 102 minutes apart, depending on the size of the previous eruption: bigger eruptions have longer intervals between them. The largest geyser in the park is called Steamboat Geyser.

TELL ME WHICH : HISTORY

WHICH COUNTRY LED THE INDUSTRIAL REVOLUTION?

Ironworks at Coalbrookdale in Shropshire

One of the biggest changes in the history of the world, the Industrial Revolution, started in Britain in the late 18th century. As the 'Workshop of the World' Britain was the first home of new machines, new types of materials and new ways of making power. This was the age of coal and iron, of gas and electricity, of railways and factories. These factories created millions of new jobs, so many people began to leave the countryside to work in the towns. Houses and factories had to be built for them. By 1850, over 60% of Britons lived in towns. Factory workers led hard lives, often working 14 hours a day, six days a week.

FACT FILE

Raw cotton, grown mainly in the United States, was very difficult and slow to clean. Whitney's cotton gin was a simple machine, which brushed out the seeds from the cotton.

In which city would you find Big Ben?

You'll find Big Ben in London, the capital city of England. It is one of the country's most famous landmarks. Most people think Big Ben is a tower, but actually it is the name of the largest bell in the Clock Tower (sometimes called St Stephen's Tower) of the Palace of Westminster, where the United Kingdom's Houses of Parliament sit. The Palace of Westminster was rebuilt after a fire in 1834 destroyed almost all of its predecessor. The clock was installed in 1854 and the tower was finished in 1858. When the original 14.5-tonne bell was tested, it broke in half and had to be recast as a 12.5-tonne (13.7 ton) bell, which, although cracked, is still in use today. If it were not for all London's traffic noise, the bell could be heard chiming 15 km (9 miles) away.

FACT FILE

Some clocks register time on a 24-hour basis. On such a clock, 9 a.m. would be shown as 0900 and 3 p.m. would be 1500. This system avoids confusion between the morning and evening hours.

IN WHICH CITY WOULD YOU FIND LIBERTY ISLAND?

Liberty Island is in New York Harbor, near Manhattan Island. It is known all over the world because it is the site of the Statue of Liberty, which was designed by Frédéric Auguste Bartholdi and built by Gustav Eiffel in the 1880s as a present from the French people to commemorate the United States' Declaration of Independence a century before. The statue, which is made of plates of copper on a steel frame, is 46 m (151 ft) tall and weighs 185 tonnes (204 tons). The statue stands in the remains of Fort

Wood, an early 19th-century fort. The fort was declared a national monument in 1924, and the rest of the island was included in the monument in 1937. The Statue of Liberty overlooks Ellis Island, which was the main point of immigration for hundreds of thousands of people from Europe and Africa during the 19th and early 20th centuries. The statue's full title is *Liberty Enlightens the World*, reflecting the long-held American belief that they should be an example and a force for good in the world.

FACT FILE

The people of France gave the Statue of Liberty to the people of the United States in 1884. This gift was an expression of friendship and of the ideal of liberty shared by both countries.

WHICH EVENT LED TO THE EASTER RISING?

In 1870, a movement calling for Home Rule was founded in Ireland. Supporters of Home Rule wanted a separate parliament to deal with Irish affairs in Dublin. Prime Minister William Gladstone was a staunch supporter of Home Rule, but he failed to get his Home Rule Bill approved by parliament.

During World War I, the issue of Home Rule continued to cause conflict in Ireland. When war actually broke out in 1914, most Irish Volunteers supported Britain in its fight against the Central Powers. But a breakaway group formed the Irish Republican Brotherhood (later known as the IRA). On Easter Monday, 1916, protesters belonging to this and other nationalist movements seized buildings in Dublin and proclaimed Ireland a republic. This rebellion became known as the Easter Rising.

FACT FILE

Irish politician Charles Parnell addresses an audience in support of Home Rule. He became leader of the Home Rule Party in the British parliament and fought tirelessly for his beliefs.

WHICH EVENT TRIGGERED WORLD WAR I?

As the 19th century drew to a close, there was an increase in rivalry between the different nations of Europe. They competed for control of colonies, and for industrial and military power. In 1882, Germany, Austria–Hungary and Italy (known as the Central Powers) formed an alliance called the Triple Alliance, promising to protect each other in the event of an attack. In 1904, Britain joined with France in a similar alliance. They were joined by Russia in 1907 to form the Triple Entente. In 1914 Archduke Franz Ferdinand of Austria-Hungary was assassinated in Serbia, activating the alliance agreements. Soon all the major European powers were drawn into conflict. Russia, backed by France, supported Serbia. Then Germany invaded neutral Belgium and attacked France, drawing Britain into the conflict.

- ■ Central Powers
- ■ Green: Allies
- □ White: Neutral Powers

FACT FILE

The Versailles Treaty ended World War I, but its terms were so severe that Germany suffered economic collapse and this caused resentment that was to build up and eventually contribute to the causes of World War II.

WHICH MACHINES MADE THEIR DEBUT IN WORLD WAR I?

World War I was the first mechanized war in history. In the beginning, fighting was similar to wars fought in the previous century. But new and terrifying weapons were introduced that completely changed the whole style of warfare. Aircraft were used for the first time to observe the enemy and to locate suitable targets for the long-range artillery. Later on, fighter planes began to shoot down the spotters, introducing aerial warfare. Aircraft and Zeppelin airships were used as bombers. The most terrifying new weapon was poison gas, which was used by both sides. It caused millions of deaths and terrible suffering. Tanks also made their first appearance.

FACT FILE

The World War I (1914–18) brought the first appearance of armoured tanks in battle. They were able to break through enemy lines and create openings for troops to advance through. Earlier use of tanks could have saved lives and helped shorten the war.

WHICH FOUR WORLD LEADERS SIGNED THE TREATY OF VERSAILLES?

FACT FILE

The signing of the Treaty of Versailles on 28 June 1919, in Paris was the fifth anniversary of the shooting of Archduke Ferdinand in Sarajevo.

The Treaty of Versailles was a peace document signed at the end of World War I by the Allied and Associated Powers and by Germany. It took place in the Hall of Mirrors in the Palace of Versailles, France, on 28 June 1919 and actually came into force on 10 January 1920. The treaty was drafted and signed during the Paris Peace Conference in the spring of 1919, which was dominated by the national leaders known as the 'Big Four', David Lloyd George of Britain, Georges Clemenceau of France, Woodrow Wilson of the United States and Vittorio Orlando of Italy. They wanted to make sure that Germany would never again pose a military threat.

WHICH EVENT TRIGGERED WORLD WAR II?

As in World War I some international alliances were activated following the German invasion of Poland. As a result of this Britain and France declared war on Germany. When the Germans attacked Poland, the Russians also attacked the country and it was divided.

The Germans went on to invade Denmark, Norway, Belgium, the Netherlands and France in quick succession. They crushed any resistance with overwhelming armoured forces.

World War II killed more people than any other war in history. The fighting spread to nearly every part of the world and included nearly 60 nations. The Americans entered the war in 1941 after being attacked by Germany's ally Japan. At this time a huge military build-up began in England.

FACT FILE

Britain was led through World War II by Winston Churchill. He is remembered for his great wartime leadership qualities and for his famous 'V for victory' sign.

WHICH EVENT ENDED WORLD WAR II?

In August 1945, the United States effectively brought the war against Japan, and therefore World War II, to a catastrophic end when it dropped two atomic bombs on the Japanese cities of Nagasaki and Hiroshima. An estimated 130,000 people were killed and many more suffered terrible after effects.

Technological advances in the machines and weapons of war had been rapid during the 20th century. During World War I, inventions included the tank and the fighter aircraft. At sea, one of the major advances in military marine technology happened before the war, with the building of the battleship *Dreadnought*. During World War II, the Germans began a new type of heavily armed warfare: Blitzkrieg or lightning war. But ultimately, the most significant and horrific development in modern warfare came with the invention of the atomic bomb in the United States. The first atomic bomb was exploded in an experiment in New Mexico, in the United States, in July 1945.

FACT FILE

During the war, Hitler tried to invade Britain. He first needed to gain control of the skies. The Battle of Britain began in July 1940 between the German Luftwaffe and Britain's RAF. By May 1941 the RAF had gained the upper hand.

WHICH PRESIDENT LED THE UNITED STATES OUT OF THE GREAT DEPRESSION?

A disastrous stock market crash in 1929 in the United States left many people penniless overnight. The effects of the Wall Street Crash were felt all over the world. Many countries in Europe were hard hit because they had borrowed money from the United States at the end of World War I. Throughout the 1930s, unemployment soared and trade slumped in a period known as the Great Depression. During the worst years of the depression, many people were forced to rely on charity and government handouts for their most basic needs. In 1932 Franklin D Roosevelt was elected US present. His 'New Deal' aimed to create jobs and to protect people's savings by regulating banks more closely. The US economy went from strength to strength from 1933 to 1937 and was boosted once more when meeting demands servicing World War II.

FACT FILE

This is the Stock Exchange in Wall Street at the time of its collapse. You can see brokers spilling out onto the streets of the city of New York.

WHICH EVENT SPARKED THE CUBAN MISSILE CRISIS?

In 1949, the Western Allies formed the North Atlantic Treaty Organization (NATO) for defence against the communist presence in Europe. In the same year, the Soviet Union exploded its first atomic bomb. With both superpowers holding nuclear weapons, fear and mistrust between the two sides increased. The Soviets constructed a wall across Berlin in 1961, separating East from West in the city. In 1962, the Cuban crisis erupted when the United States discovered that the Soviet Union was building missile sites on the island of Cuba in the Caribbean. These sites were within range to launch an attack by nuclear weapons on American cities. The two superpowers came to the brink of war before the Soviet Union agreed to withdraw the weapons. Although the two superpowers never became involved in direct warfare, both sides became involved in wars elsewhere in the world. The United States fought communism and the Soviet Union helped communist fighters.

FACT FILE

John Fitzgerald Kennedy was US president from 1961 until he was assassinated in 1963. During his presidency the Berlin Wall was built, dividing the city in two and stopping East Germans escaping communist rule.

WHICH ASSOCIATION HELPS TO KEEP THE PEACE?

This association is called the United Nations (UN) and it is led by a powerful Security Council, which can intervene in international disputes that might lead to conflict. Today the UN is also involved in many economic aid programmes around the world. During World War II the Allied nations referred to themselves as the 'United Nations'. In 1942 they agreed that they would not make any separate peace agreements with Germany. It was the Potsdam Conference in 1945 that really laid the ground for the foundation of the United Nations to prevent future conflict and also set out procedures for the prosecution of Nazi war criminals. Twenty-seven countries signed this first agreement and in 1945, after the war, the United Nations formally came into existence with an initial membership of 50 countries.

FACT FILE

Early in 1945 the Allied leaders met in Yalta in the Crimea to decide on the postwar shape of the world. Churchill, Roosevelt and Stalin decided on how Germany was to be split up once the war was won.

SCIENCE AND TECHNOLOGY

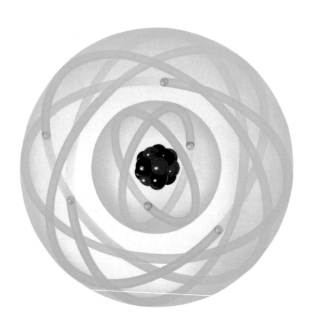

Contents

WHICH SCIENCE INVOLVES THE STUDY OF DINOSAURS? 114
WHICH CIVILIZATION INTRODUCED FIREWORKS AND GUNPOWDER? 115

WHICH CIVILIZATION MADE THE FIRST PAPER? 116
WHICH CIVILIZATION WAS THE FIRST TO USE GLASS? 117

WHICH ACID HELPS PLANTS TO GROW? 118
WHICH PROCESSES CAUSE POLLUTION? 119

WHICH US POLITICIAN INVENTED THE LIGHTNING ROD? 120
WHICH PLANE HAS NO ENGINE? 121

WHICH DEVICE USES SOUND WAVES TO FIND THINGS UNDER WATER? 122
WHICH GADGET IS USED TO MEASURE AN EARTHQUAKE? 123

WHICH MACHINES HAVE PERISCOPES? 124
WHICH MACHINES HAVE GEARS? 125

WHICH MACHINES HAVE A TRANSISTOR? 126
WHICH INVENTION HELPED ASTRONOMERS SEE INTO SPACE? 127

WHICH CODE REVOLUTIONIZED THE TELEGRAPH? 128
WHICH SYSTEM HELPS BLIND PEOPLE TO READ AND WRITE? 129

WHICH GADGET HELPS SCIENTISTS TO SEE SUPER-TINY THINGS? 130
WHICH RADIO RUNS WITHOUT ELECTRICITY? 131

WHICH METHOD OF DETECTION USES MICROWAVES? 132
WHICH DEVICE WOULD YOU FIND IN THE MOUTHPIECE OF A PHONE? 133

WHICH BEAM OF LIGHT CAN CUT METAL? 134
WHICH PLASTIC IS RESISTANT TO HEAT? 135

WHICH MATERIALS RUST? 136
WHICH PROCESS IS USED TO SPLIT AN ATOM? 137

WHICH MACHINES HAVE CATALYTIC CONVERTERS? 138
WHICH PROCESS REUSES EVERYDAY WASTE? 139

WHICH GAS IS SUPER LIGHT? 140
WHICH COUNTRY PRODUCES THE MOST CLOCKS? 141

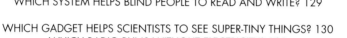
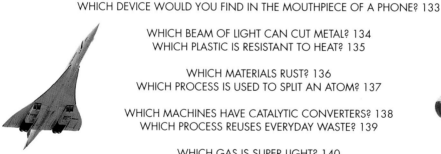

WHICH SCIENCE INVOLVES THE STUDY OF DINOSAURS?

The science that involves the study of dinosaurs is called palaeontology. Fossils, the remains of life of the past, have been found just about everywhere that there are deposits of sedimentary rocks. Dinosaurs, the spectacular and popular inhabitants of the past world, are a very rare part of this fossil treasure trove. Nevertheless, they have been found on all the continents of the Earth. The excavation of their remains is a very specialist task. Once found,

a dinosaur skeleton is excavated. First, the layers of rock above it are removed to reveal the whole thing. Then the individual bones of the fossil are mapped to mark where they lie. The bones are then sealed in a layer of plaster to protect them and transported back to the laboratory. Once in the laboratory, the specimens are prepared for further study.

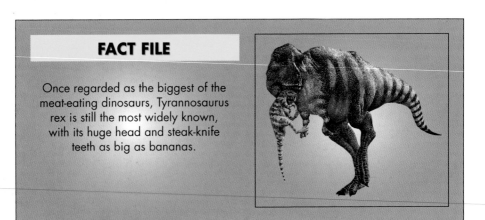

FACT FILE

Once regarded as the biggest of the meat-eating dinosaurs, Tyrannosaurus rex is still the most widely known, with its huge head and steak-knife teeth as big as bananas.

WHICH CIVILIZATION INTRODUCED FIREWORKS AND GUNPOWDER?

The earliest known fireworks can be traced back to around 2,000 years ago, and the Chinese, who first made fire crackers at this time. They are still used in China and throughout the East to celebrate weddings, births and religious festivals. In some places they are used to scare away evil spirits.

The Chinese were also the first to use gunpowder in warfare. By the year 1232, the Chinese had discovered black powder (gunpowder) and had learned to use it to make explosive bombs as well as propelling forces for rockets. Drawings made in military documents later show powder rockets tied to arrows and spears. When the Mongols laid siege to the city of K'ai-feng, the capital of Honan province, the Chinese defenders used weapons that were described as 'arrows of flying fire'. In the same battle, it is reported, the defenders dropped from the walls of the city a kind of bomb described as 'heaven-shaking thunder'.

FACT FILE

Guy Fawkes is best known for his efforts to blow up the Houses of Parliament in London, in 1605. This became known as the 'Gunpowder Plot'. His plan, however, was foiled and he was consequently arrested on 4 November 1605.

WHICH CIVILIZATION MADE THE FIRST PAPER?

The first people to use a form of paper for keeping records and correspondence were the ancient Egyptians more than 5,500 years ago. They layered strips of the stems of the papyrus plant (*Cyperis papryus*), crushed them and hammered them to form a loose-textured writing material. Before this, people in Mesopotamia had used a sharp stylus to make symbols and letters in tablets of clay. Their form of writing is known as cuneiform, while the Egyptian script developed into hieroglyphics. The first people to make paper by a simplified version of the process that is still used today were the Chinese, who about 2,000 years ago learned to crush hemp and parts of the mulberry tree to a pulp to separate out the fibres, which were then cleaned and made into thin sheets and dried. Later improvements include adding a filler such as china clay to make the surface smooth.

FACT FILE

The first person to develop a process for making paper in rolls rather than sheets was Nicholas Louis Robert, who designed a machine to do this in 1798.

WHICH CIVILIZATION WAS THE FIRST TO USE GLASS?

Glass was probably first used as a glaze on pottery to waterproof it, but the first glass vessels were made in about 1,500 BCE in Mesopotamia (modern Iraq) and Egypt. Bits of highly decorative glass vessels have been found in some tombs in the Valley of the Kings in Egypt, including a late-15th-century BCE

bottle in the tomb of Amenhopis II. At this time glass vessels were formed around a core that was then removed as the technique of blowing glass had not been invented. The Egyptians also used coloured glass inlays on the coffins and mummy cases of pharoahs and other important people, as can be seen on the gold mask of Tutankhamen. The Romans learned how to make blow pipes, and so blown glass, in about 30 BCE, which made glass vessels both easier and cheaper to manufacture. Interestingly, although it appears solid, glass is, in fact, a liquid that has been cooled very quickly to prevent it forming crystals. It moves very slowly, but glass windows that are very old are thicker at the bottom because gravity has gradually pulled the glass down.

FACT FILE

It is very easy to recycle glass. It is simply broken up and melted, before being shaped again in the normal way.

WHICH ACID HELPS PLANTS TO GROW?

There is an acid that is produced naturally, in large quantities, during thunderstorms and which falls to the Earth in rain. This acid is nitric acid, and its production during thunderstorms allows nitrogen from the air to become part of the soil in a form that plants can use. Nitric acid was one of the first acids known. Many alchemists of the Middle Ages used it in their experiments. Nitric acid is a strong inorganic acid that has many industrial uses. Its principal use is for the production of fertilizers and explosives.

FACT FILE

Nitric acid is such a powerful oxidizing agent that it dissolves many metals. But it does not attack gold and platinum. A drop of nitric acid on a ring or brooch tells whether it is made of genuine gold or platinum.

WHICH PROCESSES CAUSE POLLUTION?

Pollution is the name we give to waste products that enter the air, soil and water, but cannot be quickly broken down naturally. The processes that cause most pollution are all manmade and involve emissions from factories and cars among other things. They affect the health of plants and animals, including humans, and the environments in which they live.

It is important, as far as possible, to use materials that can break down in the soil when they are thrown away. Such materials are said to be biodegradable. One of the saddest sights is that of dead fish floating on the water. One of the most frequent ways they are killed is when the water is polluted by chemicals.

FACT FILE

Rivers and canals are often used as unofficial dumping sites for household waste. To improve matters, there are new laws to protect the environment. But we all need to help to keep the environment clean and healthy.

WHICH US POLITICIAN INVENTED THE LIGHTNING ROD?

The lightning conductor – a strip of copper that is run from the top of a building to the ground in order that lightning can earth itself safely – was the brainchild of Benjamin Franklin (1706–1790). Franklin was a printer, scientist and politician who played an important part in founding the United States. He discovered the nature of lightning while flying a kite during a thunderstorm. Franklin noticed sparks jumping from a key tied to

the end of the wet string. Lightning is a significant weather hazard and occurs at an average rate of 50 to 100 discharges per second. Lightning rods and metallic conductors can be used to protect a structure by intercepting and diverting the lightning current into the ground as harmlessly as possible.

FACT FILE

A lightning conductor is a metal rod that is placed so that it points upwards above the highest point of a tall building. If lightning does strike the building, it is the conductor, not the building that the spark hits.

WHICH PLANE HAS NO ENGINE?

A plane with no engine is called a glider. During the late 18th century, people made the first flights in the air using balloons, which were an early form of airship. After the first balloon flights, inventors tried to develop a heavier-than-air flying machine. Some inventors experimented with gliders. They studied birds' wings and discovered that the wings were curved. By building gliders with curved wings instead of flat ones, they could make the vehicles fly hundreds of metres. But long-distance flight in a heavier-than-air machine did not become possible until the invention of an engine light enough but powerful enough to keep a plane in flight. The first such engines were four-stroke gasoline engines, developed during the 1880s and initially used to power bicycles, boats and carriages.

FACT FILE

In 1903, the brothers Orville and Wilbur Wright – two American bicycle makers – made the first successful powered aeroplane flights in history near Kitty Hawk, North Carolina.

WHICH DEVICE USES SOUND WAVES TO FIND THINGS UNDER WATER?

Sound waves travel through water, and can be used to detect submarines or wrecks on the seafloor. Fishermen even use them to find shoals of fish. They do so by using a sonar device. Here's how it works: a sonar device under a ship sends out sound waves that travel down through the water. The sound waves are then reflected back from any solid object they reach, such as shoals of fish or something on the seabed. The echoes are received by the ship and can be used to 'draw' an image of the object, and its location, onto a computer screen.

Sonar, or echo sounding, is used by fishermen to detect shoals of fish. It can also be used to detect submarines or to find wrecks on the seafloor.

sound waves transmitted from ship

sound waves reflected from fish

FACT FILE

Concorde was an aircraft that actually broke the sound barrier and was the only supersonic airliner in regular use. When travelling at such very high speeds, an aircraft begins to build up a huge wave of compressed air in front of it causing a sonic 'boom'.

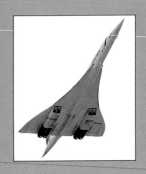

WHICH GADGET IS USED TO MEASURE AN EARTHQUAKE?

Every 30 seconds, somewhere on this planet, the ground suddenly rumbles and trembles. Most of the movements are so slight that they are not felt. Others can be so large they cause complete disaster. Big cracks appear in the land, streets buckle and buildings simply crumble. In fact whole towns and cities can be destroyed. These are called earthquakes and the reason they occur is because the Earth's crust is made up of moving parts called

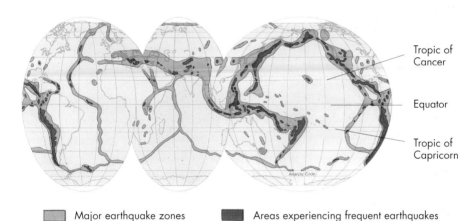

Tropic of Cancer

Equator

Tropic of Capricorn

Major earthquake zones   Areas experiencing frequent earthquakes

FACT FILE

The edges of the Pacific plate are surrounded by earthquakes, volcanic activity and hot springs, caused by the crust shifts and hot lava rises near the surface.

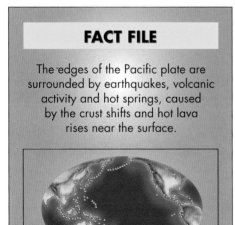

plates. When these plates slide past or into each other, the rocks jolt and send out shock waves. This is an earthquake.

The study of earthquakes is called seismology, and scientists who record earthquakes use a device called a seismograph. This special gadget picks up the vibrations that are caused by one rock mass rubbing against another. The energy of this rubbing is changed to vibration in the rocks. This vibration can travel many thousands of miles.

WHICH MACHINES HAVE PERISCOPES?

Periscopes are most commonly associated with submarines, but they can also be used by tanks, military helicopters and individuals. The simplest version is a tube with one opening at the top front and another at the bottom rear. Inside are two mirrors, set at 45 degrees to the tube and parallel to each other. An image of what the top opening of the periscope is pointed at is reflected from the top mirror down to the bottom mirror and then out of the lower opening so that the viewer can see it. In a battle, this allows the viewer to see over the top of walls or trees so he can shoot at the opposition without exposing himself to their fire. This simple sort of periscope was used in the trenches in northern Europe in World War I.

Submarine periscopes are more complicated as they have prisms instead of mirrors and lenses that magnify the image. Tank and helicopter periscopes can both be rotated through 360 degrees. Some modern submarines use electronic imaging techniques instead of mechanical periscopes.

FACT FILE

The armed forces also use helicopters to observe the movements of enemy troops and ships. Many naval helicopters have devices to locate and track submarines.

WHICH MACHINES HAVE GEARS?

Many mechanical pieces have gears – from watches to bicycles to cars. A gear is a mechanical device that transfers rotating motion and power from one part of a machine to another. Gears are produced in a wide range of sizes, and they vary greatly in use. They range from the tiny gears that drive the hands of a watch to the huge gears that turn the propeller of a supertanker. A simple gear consists of a metal wheel or disc with slots called teeth around the edge. Gears always work in pairs. The teeth of one

FACT FILE

A bicycle's gear system makes pedalling easier at certain times. Low gears, which make it easy to pedal up hills or against the wind, rotate the rear wheel only a little bit during each turn of the pedals.

gear mesh (fit together) with the teeth of the other gear. Each gear has a metal axle in the middle. The axle of one gear is connected to a power source, such as an electric motor. When the power axle turns, its gear turns and causes the second gear to rotate in the opposite direction. This action powers the axle of the second gear to do useful work.

WHICH MACHINES HAVE A TRANSISTOR?

A transistor is a tiny device that controls the flow of electric current and it is found in radios, television sets, computers and almost every other kind of electronic equipment. Transistors vary in size tremendously. Transistors are the main components built into computer chips. Some chips no larger than a fingernail contain millions of transistors. A transistor has two basic functions: (1) to switch electric current on and off and (2) to amplify or strengthen electric current.

Transistors replaced electronic components called vacuum tubes almost completely in the 1950s and 1960s because they have a number of advantages over vacuum tubes. For example, transistors are smaller, lighter, less expensive to produce, cheaper to operate, and more reliable than vacuum tubes.

FACT FILE

The ability to amplify signals makes transistors essential parts of radios and television sets. The broadcast waves that travel through the air generate weak currents in a radio or TV antenna. Transistors amplify these signals to produce sounds and pictures.

WHICH INVENTION HELPED ASTRONOMERS SEE INTO SPACE?

For centuries skywatchers looked to the heavens and asked questions about the planets and stars they could see with the naked eye. Then, in the 17th century, curiosity drove astronomers to develop the telescope, enabling them to study the stars and the planets in much more detail. In 1608 Dutch spectacle maker Hans Lippey developed a refracting telescope. Refracting telescopes work by having a convex lens, which bends light rays from an object to form an upside-down image of the object. A second lens, the eyepiece, bends the rays again and magnifies the image. In 1668, English mathematician Issac Newton developed the reflecting telescope. A reflecting telescope uses a shaped primary mirror to reflect light to a smaller secondary mirror. The light is then reflected to the focus and the image is viewed through an eyepiece.

Newton's telescope

FACT FILE

The Hubble Space Telescope was launched in 1990 and orbits Earth at around 600 km (370 miles) above the surface. This is a reflecting telescope, and is powered by two solar panels. Hubble is designed to look a long way beyond the Solar System. The volume of space it can cover is 350 times bigger than can be seen from the Earth.

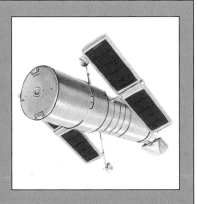

WHICH CODE REVOLUTIONIZED THE TELEGRAPH?

The invention of the telegraph meant that news could get to anywhere in the world much more quickly than had been possible ever before. In 1840, the American inventor Samuel Morse launched a code that speeded up the process even more. Known as Morse code, this revolutionary system was based on dots, dashes and spaces. Morse first got his idea for the code in 1832 when he was told about experiments with electricity. His idea was to develop a code based on interrupting the flow of electricity so that a message could be heard. Morse code works very simply. Electricity is either switched on or off. When it is on, it travels along a wire. At the other end of the wire the electric current can either make a sound or be printed out. A short electric current, a 'dit', is printed as a dot and a longer 'dah' is printed as a dash. The full Morse code is based on combining dots and dashes to represent the letters of the alphabet.

FACT FILE

The telegraph was invented in 1794 by Claude Chappe. France was at war at the time and a quick way to warn of an invasion was needed. Chappe's telegraph used two arms at the top of a tall tower. Ropes and pulleys moved the arms into different positions each representing a letter. The towers were positioned 10 to 30 km (6 to 18 miles) apart and the messages were read by people using telescopes.

WHICH SYSTEM HELPS BLIND PEOPLE TO READ AND WRITE?

In 1829 a blind gentleman called Louis Braille developed a system that would allow blind people to read and write. The system was named after him and is today one of the most widely used alphabets for the blind. The Braille system consists of dots. Each letter of the alphabet is represented by a combination of dots. These combinations are punched onto paper, so that they appear as raised bumps. A blind person reads the dots by moving their fingers over the bumps, recognizing each letter to spell out the words.

The tip of the finger 'feels' the Braille letters.

FACT FILE

Semaphore is a means of communicating by using flags. Different flag positions represent different letters and numbers. It was widely used between ships sailing near each other in the days before radio.

There were earlier systems of reading for the blind. Even as far back as 1517, alphabetic letters were engraved onto blocks of wood for the blind to read. This system was good to read by, but the drawback was that the blind could not see how to form the letters when they wanted to write.

WHICH GADGET HELPS SCIENTISTS TO SEE SUPER-TINY THINGS?

The gadget is a microscope and it allows scientists to see things that are invisible to the naked eye. The word microscope is a combination of two Greek words, *mikros* or 'small' and *skopos* or 'watcher'. So this means that a microscope is a 'watcher of small' objects. Normally an object appears larger the closer it is brought to the human eye. But when it is nearer than 25.5 cm (10 in) it becomes blurred. It is said to be out of focus. Now if a simple convex lens is placed between the eye and the object, the object can be brought nearer than 25.5 cm (10 in) and still remain in focus. Today the microscope is important to man in almost every form of industry.

It was a Dutchman called Antonie van Leeuwenhoek (1632–1723) who discovered ground glass lenses, which he used to examine the world about him. In the 1670s he made his first crude microscope with a tiny lens. This allowed him to be the first person to see microscopic life such as bacteria.

FACT FILE

Some microscopes are so powerful they can magnify the smallest objects many thousands of times. This plant cell would be invisible to the human eye without the use of magnification.

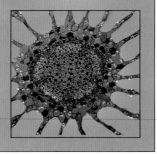

WHICH RADIO RUNS WITHOUT ELECTRICITY?

In 1991, British inventor Trevor Baylis invented a portable wind-up radio, enabling millions in the developing world, with no permanent electricity supply, to receive broadcasts. The radio works, not on electricity, but by winding up a spring, which slowly uncoils and powers a small generator.

The portable radio was invented in 1947. The invention was made possible by the development of a device called a transistor, which replaced the valves inside radios that picked up radio signals. Transistors were much smaller than valves, so it now became possible to make portable radios. In 1955 a Japanese company called Tokyo Tsushin Kogyo decided to build a portable radio for the US market. Before they began to sell the radio, they changed the company name to something Americans could say easily – the new company name was Sony.

FACT FILE

On 18 October 1954 the world's 'first pocket radio' went on sale. The Regency TR1 is just 12 cm (4¾ in) high. Around 100,000 TR1s sold during the radio's only year of production.

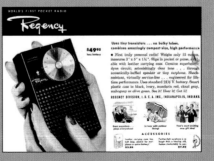

WHICH METHOD OF DETECTION USES MICROWAVES?

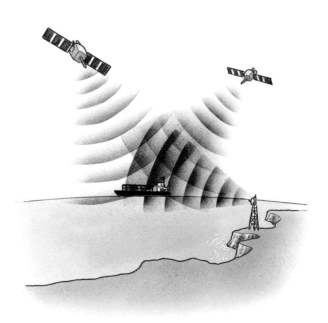

Radar uses microwave radiation to detect distant objects. The microwaves usually scan round in a circle, and the echoes sent back produce an image on a screen. Radar is a scientific method used to detect and locate moving or fixed objects. Radar can determine the direction, distance, height and speed of objects that are much too far away for the human eye to see. It can find objects as small as insects or as large as mountains. Radar can even operate well at night and in heavy fog, rain or snow. Almost every radar set works by sending radio waves towards an object and receiving the waves that are reflected from the object. The time it takes for the reflected waves to return indicates the object's range – how far away it is. The direction from which the reflected waves return tells the object's location.

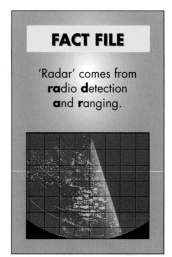

FACT FILE

'Radar' comes from **ra**dio **d**etection **a**nd **r**anging.

WHICH DEVICE WOULD YOU FIND IN THE MOUTHPIECE OF A PHONE?

A carbon transmitter is found in the handset of a landline telephone. It involves a microphone, which produces an electric copy of the user's voice, and a receiver, which duplicates the voice of the person on the other end of the line.

Mobile phones are two-way radios that convert the sound to radio waves, which travel through the air until they reach a receiver at a nearby base station. The base station sends your call through the network until it reaches the person you are calling. When you get a call, a nearby base station sends out radio waves that are detected by your mobile, where the signals are converted into voice or data.

FACT FILE

Alexander Graham Bell (1847–1922), a Scottish-born inventor and educator, is best known for his invention of the telephone. Bell was 27 years old when he worked out the principle of transmitting speech electrically, and was 29 when his basic telephone patent was granted in 1876.

WHICH BEAM OF LIGHT CAN CUT METAL?

When used as a laser, it is possible for a narrow beam of extremely strong light to cut metal. The word laser stands for **l**ight **a**mplification by **s**timulated **e**mission of **r**adiation and the first model was built in 1960 by scientist Theodore Maiman,

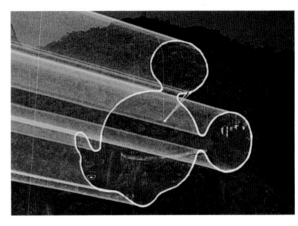

who used a rod-shaped crystal of synthetic ruby to produce a very bright, very narrow beam of light. Lasers amplify light by causing photons to be bounced back and forth in a substance (which can be solid, liquid or gas), which add extra energy. The result is that intense light is emitted in a very narrow beam. The intense beam of light produced by a laser can be used to produce images for publicity or entertainment purposes. Lasers are also used to cut metal, and for precision cuts in operations. In CD players laser light is scanned across the CD's silvery surface, reading the tiny changes in light reflected back. They are also used in office printers and scanners. In engineering, the intense narrow beam of light is used to measure and align roads and tunnels.

FACT FILE

Lasers are used everyday in our shops and banks to scan banknotes to see whether they are forgeries. This is done by passing the note under an ultraviolet light scanner.

WHICH PLASTIC IS RESISTANT TO HEAT?

All plastics belong to one of two basic types, based on how they behave when heated. These types are: thermosetting plastics and thermoplastics. Thermoplastics are the ones that are resistant to heat. They can be melted and re-formed again and again. Their polymer chains do not form cross-links. So, the chains can move freely each time the plastic material is heated. Thermoplastics are widely used because they are easier to handle. They also require less time to set.

Thermoplastics can be dispersed in liquids to produce durable, high-gloss paints and lacquers. Because their molecules can slide slowly past one another, some thermoplastics tend to lose their shape when exposed to constant pressure over a long period of time. Polytetrafluoroethylene is a thermoplastic that resists heat and chemicals and slides easily. It is used for cable insulation, bearings, valve seats, gaskets and frying pan coatings.

FACT FILE

Products made from thermosetting plastics include pot handles, trays for sterilizing medical instruments and parts for aeroplanes and spacecraft.

WHICH MATERIALS RUST?

Rust is a brownish-red substance that forms on the surface of iron or steel when it is exposed to damp air. The term used alone means iron rust, which consists mainly of hydrated iron oxide. Rust is formed by the union of oxygen in the air with iron by a process called oxidation. Rust not only corrodes the surface but also weakens the metal. Long exposure to air and moisture will cause nails to rust off, and rust holes to form in sheet iron. Iron can be mixed with other chemical elements to create rust-resistant metals called stainless steels. Iron and steel that are not rust resistant should be kept dry or coated with a substance, such as chrome or paint, that will resist the action of oxygen. Polished tools may be easily protected if wiped with a cloth soaked in oil. Coating metal objects with heavy greases or spray-on plastics, or wrapping them in special chemically treated paper, also prevents rust.

FACT FILE

You would not want to eat with rusty cutlery, so chromium is added to steel to make an alloy called stainless steel. Unlike other metals, stainless steel will not react with acids in foods.

WHICH PROCESS IS USED TO SPLIT AN ATOM?

FACT FILE

The process by which the nucleus of an atom is split to release a large amount of energy is called fission.

The splitting of atoms was first observed under laboratory conditions in the late 1930s. On 2 December 1942, a team of scientists led by Enrico Fermi achieved the first controlled nuclear fission chain reaction. During World War II, a team of scientists in the United States worked on the Manhattan Project to design and build atom bombs. In August 1945, two atom bombs were dropped on the Japanese cities of Hiroshima and Nagasaki. Uranium fission can be contained and controlled inside a nuclear reactor to produce heat for generating electricity. The first atomic power station began operation in 1956 at Calder Hall in England. Today, the Large Hadron Collider is a devcie that uses magnetism to break atoms apart.

WHICH MACHINES HAVE CATALYTIC CONVERTERS?

A catalytic converter is a device that reduces the exhaust pollutants produced by a car's engine. The engine's combustion process gives off carbon monoxide and other harmful chemical compounds. A substance called a catalyst in the converter helps change these pollutants into safer substances. The catalyst in most converters is a blend of the metals platinum, palladium and rhodium. The catalytic converter is installed in a car's exhaust system. As the exhaust gases pass through the converter, the catalyst causes carbon monoxide and other pollutants to change to oxygen, nitrogen, water and carbon dioxide.

FACT FILE

Cars with catalytic converters must use fuel that is free of both lead and phosphorus. These substances coat the catalyst's surface, making it ineffective.

WHICH PROCESS REUSES EVERYDAY WASTE?

Recycling is the process that resuses everyday waste, such as cans, glass containers, newspapers and office paper. The process is designed to collect, process and reuse materials instead of throwing them away. Recycling programmes also collect plastics and used motor oil. Recycling helps conserve raw materials and energy that manufacturers would otherwise use to make new products. Recycling keeps materials out of landfills (areas where wastes are deposited and covered with earth or other material), saving scarce landfill space. Recycling also helps reduce the pollution that may result from waste disposal.

FACT FILE

When you buy a new car it may not be quite as new as you think. Up to 40% of the steel may have come from old cars. Recycling scrap steel saves raw materials and energy.

WHICH GAS IS SUPER LIGHT?

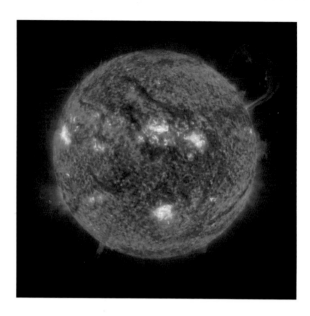

Helium is super light. On the Earth, helium comes from natural gas deposits in the atmosphere. The atmosphere contains about 5 parts of helium per million parts of air. Helium is a lightweight gas and chemical element and makes up only a small fraction of the Earth's matter. But it is one of the most common elements in the universe. The Sun and other stars are made mostly of helium and hydrogen. The energy of these stars is produced when hydrogen atoms join together to form helium atoms. Because helium is so light, it constantly escapes from the atmosphere and drifts into space. But the lost helium is replaced by radioactive minerals that shoot out alpha particles.

FACT FILE

Divers sometimes breathe a mixture of helium and oxygen to avoid a painful illness called nitrogen narcosis. Nitrogen narcosis usually occurs at depths below 30 m (100 ft).

WHICH COUNTRY PRODUCES THE MOST CLOCKS?

Grandfather clock

If we think about different types of clocks and watches, we associate some of them with different countries: grandfather clocks and marine chronometers from England, cuckoo clocks from both Germany and Switzerland, precision-engineered jewelled watches from Switzerland, too, and digital watches from countries in Southeast Asia such as Japan. Watches are very important to the Swiss economy as these expensive items are sold all over the world. Of course, many of the other items that we have in our homes also have clocks in: video recorders, DVD players, PCs, microwave ovens and cameras all tell the time. And as most of these goods are made in Southeast Asia, we can safely say that most clocks are made there.

Wristwatch

FACT FILE

The first mechanical alarm clock was invented in 1787 by a Mr Hutchins of New Hampshire, and the first wind-up alarm clock that could be set for any time was devised by a Mr Thomas in 1876.

THE HUMAN BODY

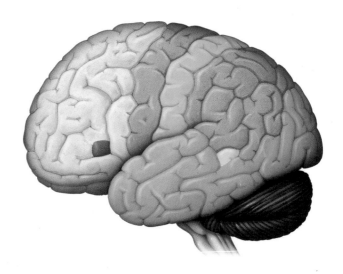

CONTENTS

WHICH WAS THE FIRST-EVER SURGICAL TREATMENT?   144
WHICH MUSCLE IN THE BODY RAISES AN EYEBROW?   145

WHICH IS THE LARGEST MUSCLE IN YOUR BODY?   146
WHICH MUSCLE HAS A STEADY BEAT?   147

WHICH PARTS OF THE BODY SEND MESSAGES?   148
WHICH NERVE IN YOUR BODY IS THE THICKEST?   149

WHICH PART OF THE BRAIN CONTROLS OUR THOUGHTS?   150
WHICH PART OF THE BODY CONTROLS TEMPERATURE?   151

WHICH BLOOD GROUP ARE YOU?   152
WHICH CELLS CARRY BLOOD AROUND YOUR BODY?   153

WHICH PROCESS PREVENTS BLOOD FLOWING BACKWARDS?   154
WHICH PROCESS STOPS WOUNDS FROM BLEEDING?   155

WHICH GLAND IS THE LARGEST?   156
WHICH MUSCLES ARE SMOOTH?   157

WHICH HORMONE IS MADE BY THE PANCREAS?   158
WHICH PART OF THE BODY STORES BILE?   159

WHICH BONES FORM YOUR PELVIS?   160
IN WHICH PART OF THE BODY WOULD YOU FIND THE METACARPALS?   161

WHICH BONES MAKE UP THE SPINE?   162
WHICH IS THE SMALLEST BONE IN YOUR BODY?   163

WHICH JOINT IN YOUR BODY IS THE BIGGEST?   164
WHICH PART OF YOUR BODY CONTROLS BALANCE?   165

WHICH PART OF THE BODY HAS FOLLICLES?   166
WHICH PART OF THE EYE LETS IN LIGHT?   167

IN WHICH PART OF THE BODY IS THE MANDIBLE?   168
WHICH CORDS HELP YOU TO SPEAK?   169

WHICH BUDS COAT YOUR TONGUE?   170
IN WHICH PART OF THE BODY DOES DIGESTION START?   171

IN WHICH PART OF THE BODY DOES DIGESTION END?   172
IN WHICH PART OF THE BODY IS THE ACHILLES TENDON?   173

WHICH PART OF THE BODY STORES URINE?   174
WHICH CELLS ARE MADE IN BONE MARROW?   175

IN WHICH PART OF THE BODY DOES SPERM DEVELOP?   176
WHICH PROCESS ENDS IN MENSTRUATION?   177

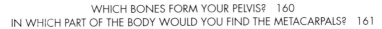

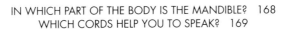
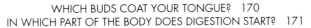

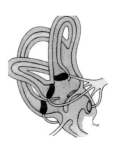

WHICH WAS THE FIRST-EVER SURGICAL TREATMENT?

In prehistoric times the first known surgical treatment was an operation called trephining. People believed that angry gods or evil spirits caused disease. Curing the sick required calming the gods or driving the evil spirits from the body. The priests who tried to soothe the gods or drive out the evil spirits became the first professional healers of the sick.

Trephining (also known as trepanning) involved using a stone instrument to cut a hole in a patient's skull.

FACT FILE

Prehistoric people probably also discovered that many plants can be used as drugs – for example, the use of quinine to prevent an illness called malaria. It is made from the bark of the cinchona tree.

Scientists have found fossils of trephined skulls as old as 10,000 years. Early people may have performed the operation to release spirits believed responsible for headaches, mental illness or epilepsy.

Trephining may have brought relief in some cases by releasing pressure in the head. Surgeons still use a similar procedure to relieve some types of pressure on the brain.

WHICH MUSCLE IN THE BODY RAISES AN EYEBROW?

Every move you make, every breath you take, every song you sing... muscles power all of your body's movements, from blinking to leaping high in the air. Muscle actions are controlled by messages travelling to them from your brain, along nerves called motor nerves. We use our muscles to communicate and send information – and not just by speaking, which uses around 40 muscles. We also use muscles to 'make faces' or facial expressions. Here are some of the 60 or so face muscles and what they do.

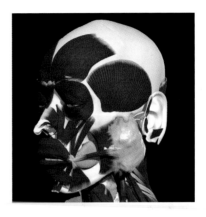

MUSCLE NAME	SITE	WHAT IT DOES	EXPRESSION
Frontalis	Forehead	Raises eyebrows	Surprise
Procerus	Between eyes	Pulls eyebrows in and down	Stern, concentration
Auricularis	Above and to side of ear	Wiggles ear	
Buccinator	Cheek	Moves cheek	Blowing, sucking
Risorius	Side of mouth	Pulls corner of mouth	Grin
Depressor labii	Under lip	Pulls lower lip down	Frown

FACT FILE

A muscle is a bundle of fibres. These bundles are called fascicles. Within each fibre is a group of fibrils. A single fibril contains myosin and actin filaments. These slide past each other to shorten the muscle.

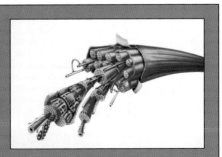

WHICH IS THE LARGEST MUSCLE IN YOUR BODY?

The largest muscle in the human body is called the gluteus maximus and this is situated in the buttocks, while the smallest is the stapedius, which can be found in the middle ear. A muscle is the tough, elastic tissue that makes body parts move. Muscles are found throughout the body. As a person grows, the muscles also get bigger. Muscle makes up nearly half the body weight of an adult. The human body has more than 600 major muscles and about 240 of them have specific names. There are two main types of muscles: (1) skeletal muscles and (2) smooth muscles. A third kind of muscle, called cardiac muscle, has characteristics of both skeletal and smooth muscles. It is found only in the heart. People use muscles to make various movements.

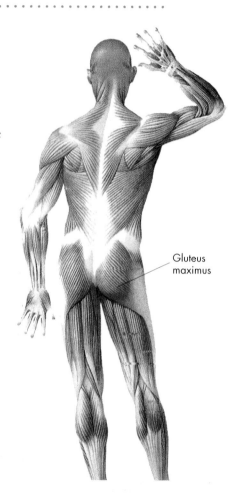

Gluteus maximus

FACT FILE

Among the most powerful muscles are the masseters, one on each side of the face. The longest muscle is the sartorius, which runs from the side of the waist, diagonally down across the front of the thigh to the inside of the knee.

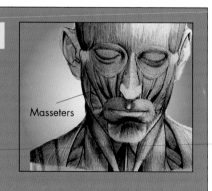

Masseters

WHICH MUSCLE HAS A STEADY BEAT?

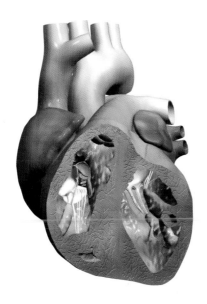

FACT FILE

The muscle that makes up the walls of the heart, called cardiac muscle or myocardium, never ceases working and needs a continuing supply of blood.

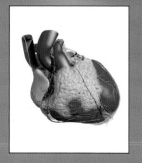

In the centre of your chest, below a thin layer of skin, muscle and bone sits your heart. Actually a muscle, this simple, yet essential, pump carries blood to and from your body's billions of cells non-stop, day and night. During an average lifetime (70 years) the heart beats 2.5 billion times. Although your heart cannot actually control whether you will fall in love or if you are a big-hearted (kind) person, without the heart's second-by-second collection and delivery service, your cells – and your body – would die.

The heart is between the lungs. It tips slightly to the left side, which is why people think it is on the left side of the body. The heart is about the size of its owner's clenched fist. As you grow from a child into an adult, your heart will grow at the same rate as your clenched fist.

WHICH PARTS OF THE BODY SEND MESSAGES?

Messages are sent to the brain from different parts of the body and back through the nerves. A nerve impulse is like a very simple message: either on or off. Because there are so many neurones connected to one another, this simple signal is enough to carry the most complicated messages throughout the whole of the body's nervous system. As a nerve impulse arrives at the junction between two nerve cells, it is carried across the gap or synapse by chemicals called neurotransmitters. These contact sensitive areas in the next nerve cell, and the nerve impulse is carried along.

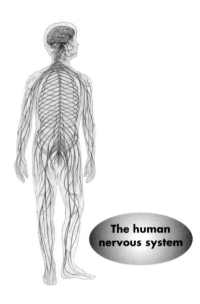

The human nervous system

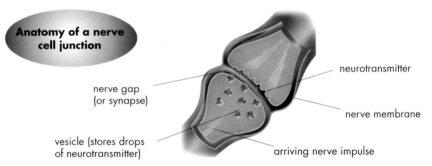

Anatomy of a nerve cell junction

nerve gap (or synapse)

neurotransmitter

vesicle (stores drops of neurotransmitter)

nerve membrane

arriving nerve impulse

FACT FILE

Scientists have produced maps showing how electrical activity in one part of the brain can cause a movement or other reaction. This mapping has been done during brain surgery. As there are no sense organs in the brain it is possible to operate on people who are fully conscious, without them feeling any pain.

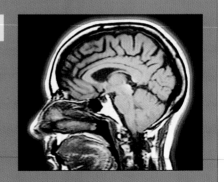

WHICH NERVE IN YOUR BODY IS THE THICKEST?

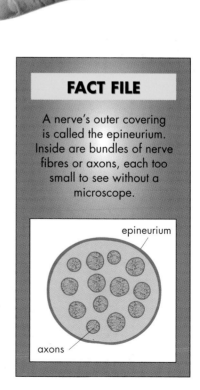

The thickest nerve in the human body is the sciatic nerve, in the hip and upper thigh. It is about the width of its owner's thumb. This is thicker than the spinal cord, which is usually the width of its owner's little finger.

Our nerve systems control our every movement and action, and every process that happens inside the body. Your nervous system is made up of your brain, spinal cord and nerves. It works by sending tiny electrical signals called nerve impulses. Millions of these travel around the body and brain every second, like the busiest computer network. When you hurt a finger you probably feel the touch first, and then the pain starts a moment later. This is because the signals about touch travel faster along the nerves than the signals about pain. There are two main nervous systems within the body. The central nervous system is the brain's main control centre. It sends nerve impulses to the rest of the body using the peripheral nervous system. We have conscious control over the central and peripheral nervous systems.

FACT FILE

A nerve's outer covering is called the epineurium. Inside are bundles of nerve fibres or axons, each too small to see without a microscope.

epineurium

axons

WHICH PART OF THE BRAIN CONTROLS OUR THOUGHTS?

Our brains have five distinct areas, each of which controls specific activities that we do from day to day. The cerebrum is the part that controls thought. A big wrinkled, dome that covers most of the top of the brain, the cerebrum forms more than four-fifths of the whole brain. It has a thin outer layer of 'grey matter', which is mainly nerve cells, covering an inner mass of 'white matter', which is chiefly nerve fibres.

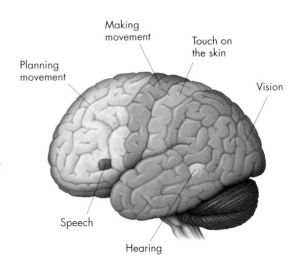

Making movement

Touch on the skin

Planning movement

Vision

Speech

Hearing

The other parts of the brain are the cerebellum, which carries out detailed control of muscles; the thalamus, which helps to sort and process information from four of the senses (eyes, ears, tongue, skin); the hypothalamus, a centre for powerful feelings, emotions and urges such as anger, fear, love and joy; and the brain stem – the base of the brain, which contains the main 'life support' areas for heartbeat, breathing, blood pressure and control of digestion. Its lower end merges into the top of the spinal cord.

FACT FILE

Even when asleep, the brain is just as active sending nerve messages around itself as it is when awake. Older people tend to sleep more hours overall but often in several sessions, such as 'cat-naps' throughout the day.

WHICH PART OF THE BODY CONTROLS TEMPERATURE?

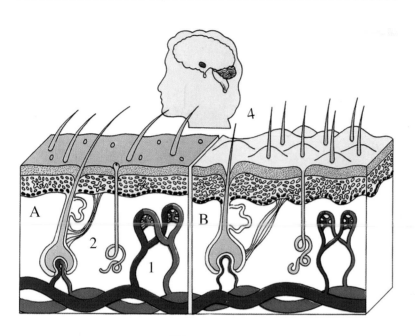

FACT FILE

Body movements can also be homeostatic. A hot person may spread out arms and legs to increase heat loss; a cold person curls up to reduce the areas of the body losing warmth.

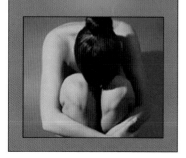

The name for 'constancy of the internal environment' is homeostasis. The body must regulate many body systems and processes to keep inner conditions stable. The temperature nucleus in the hypothalamus controls heat loss and production by the body through the skin. Overheating (A) causes an increased blood flow from the blood vessels (1), to radiate heat and causes sweating through the sweat glands (2), to lose heat. A fall in body temperature (B) constricts the surface blood vessels, stops sweating and makes the erector muscles (3) contract, causing the hairs (4) to stand on end, trapping air as an insulating layer. Additional heat can be produced by shivering.

151

WHICH BLOOD GROUP ARE YOU?

It is important to know what blood group someone is if they are about to become a donor. This is because certain kinds or groups of blood, when mixed together, may form clumps or clots, and this can be dangerous during a blood transfusion, when blood is given or donated by one person, to be put into another person, the recipient. Humans have four different blood groups, which were discovered in 1900, which can be tested using a system called ABO. A person can be either A, B, AB or O. A person with group O is a 'universal donor' whose blood can be given to almost anyone. A person with group AB is a 'universal recipient' who can receive blood from almost anyone.

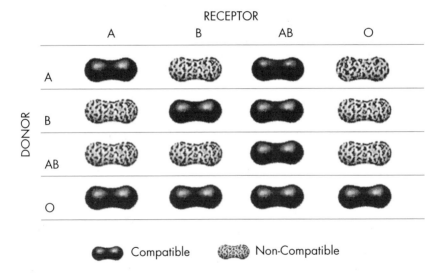

FACT FILE

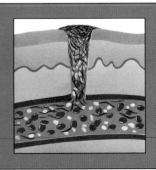

Blood begins to clot as soon as it is exposed to the air, plugging the wound. White blood cells gather around the wound to kill invading microbes, and new skin cells grow into the healing wound beneath the scab.

WHICH CELLS CARRY BLOOD AROUND YOUR BODY?

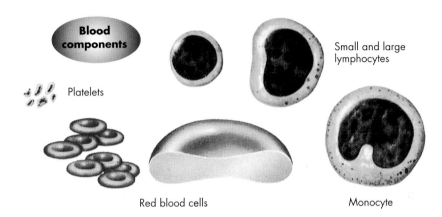

Blood components

Platelets

Small and large lymphocytes

Red blood cells

Monocyte

Red blood cells carry oxygen around the body. They are among the most numerous cells in the body, with 25,000 billion in an average person. They are also among the smallest cells in the body. Each red cell is shaped like a doughnut without the hole poked completely through and its colour is due to the substance haemoglobin. Haemoglobin joins or attaches to oxygen and carries it around the body. Each red cell contains 250 million tiny particles, or molecules, of haemoglobin. Red blood cells live for three or four months, then they die and are broken apart. This means about 3 million red blood cells die every second – and the same number of new ones are made. Red blood cells, like white blood cells and platelets, are made in the jelly-like marrow inside bones. Our blood contains millions and millions of red blood cells.

FACT FILE

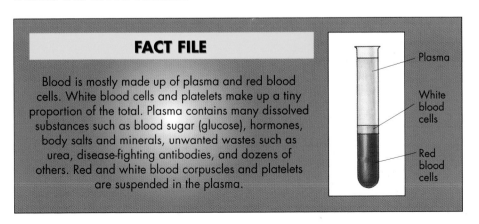

Blood is mostly made up of plasma and red blood cells. White blood cells and platelets make up a tiny proportion of the total. Plasma contains many dissolved substances such as blood sugar (glucose), hormones, body salts and minerals, unwanted wastes such as urea, disease-fighting antibodies, and dozens of others. Red and white blood corpuscles and platelets are suspended in the plasma.

Plasma

White blood cells

Red blood cells

WHICH PROCESS PREVENTS BLOOD FLOWING BACKWARDS?

Blood circulation is controlled through a series of valves in the veins. A vein is a blood vessel that carries blood towards the heart. The blood circulates in the body through a system of tubes called blood vessels. The blood in your veins travels quite slowly, and many large veins have valves to stop the blood from draining backwards towards the legs and feet. Blood flowing forwards forces the valve flaps to open (see top right). Blood flowing back forces them to shut (see bottom right). The valves in the heart work in exactly the same way. Blood is also helped along by the arm and leg muscles contracting. That is why, if you stand still for a long period of time, blood can collect in your legs and make them puffy and sore.

FACT FILE

The lymphatic system is one of the body's defences against infection. Harmful particles and bacteria that have entered the body are filtered out by small masses of tissue that lie along the lymphatic vessels. These bean-shaped masses are called lymph nodes.

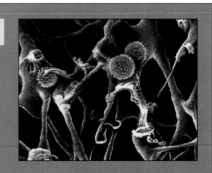

WHICH PROCESS STOPS WOUNDS FROM BLEEDING?

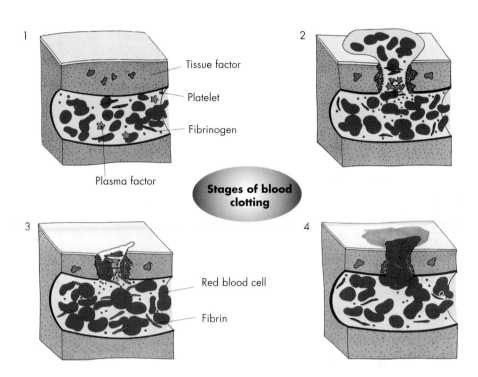

1

Tissue factor

Platelet

Fibrinogen

Plasma factor

Stages of blood clotting

3

4

Red blood cell

Fibrin

FACT FILE

Your blood pressure can be measured by a doctor with a special blood pressure monitor. During sleep your blood pressure decreases slightly, and during exercise and emotional excitement it increases.

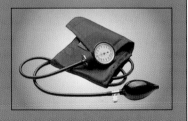

When you cut yourself, the blood clots to prevent the wound from bleeding. Clotting is caused by substances in the blood. Together with small particles called platelets, these substances produce masses of fine mesh when they are exposed to air. They block the wound and prevent more blood loss. New cells grow rapidly into the wound, replacing the damaged tissue. Soon the clotted material, called a scab, falls off and clean, new skin is revealed underneath.

WHICH GLAND IS THE LARGEST?

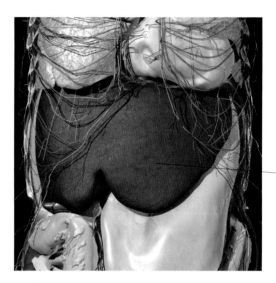

Liver

The liver is the largest gland in the human body and one of the most complex of all human organs. It serves as the body's main chemical factory and is one of its major storehouses of food. The liver is a reddish-brown mass weighing about 1.4 kg (3 lb). It is located in the upper right part of the abdomen, under the diaphragm and above the stomach and intestines. The liver performs many essential functions. One of its most important tasks is to help the body digest food. The liver produces and discharges bile, a greenish-yellow digestive fluid. Bile travels from the liver to the small intestine, where it aids in the digestion of fats. Extra bile is stored in the gallbladder, a pear-shaped pouch that lies under the liver.

FACT FILE

The liver has a remarkable ability to produce new cells to replace its own diseased or damaged cells. Surgeons can remove a section of healthy liver from an adult and transplant it into a child with a diseased liver. The child will grow healthy liver over time.

WHICH MUSCLES ARE SMOOTH?

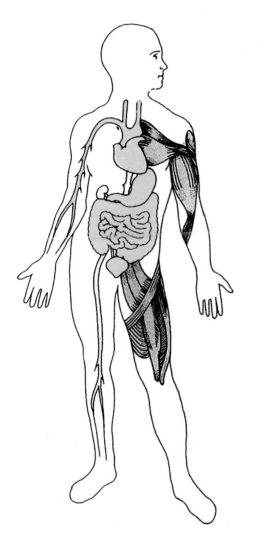

Smooth muscles can be found in the walls of the stomach, intestines, blood vessels and bladder, and because they are not consciously controlled by the brain, we also know them as involuntary muscles. They work slowly and automatically in a natural, rhythmic way, contracting then relaxing, controlling our many body processes. For example, the steady action of these muscles in the stomach and intestines move food along for digestion. Smooth muscles react to stimulus from particular nerves that are part of the autonomic nervous system, and also to the effect of certain body chemicals.

FACT FILE

Muscle cells are excitable because the membrane of each cell is electrically charged. Thus a muscle cell is said to have electric potential.

WHICH HORMONE IS MADE BY THE PANCREAS?

Insulin is a hormone produced by the pancreas. The purpose of insulin is to keep the level of sugar in the blood down to normal levels. If the level of sugar in the blood begins to rise above certain limits, the Islets of Langerhans respond by releasing insulin into the bloodstream. The insulin then acts to oppose the effects of hormones such as cortisone and adrenalin, both of which raise the level of sugar in the blood. The insulin exerts its effect by allowing sugar to pass from the bloodstream into the body's cells to be used as a fuel.

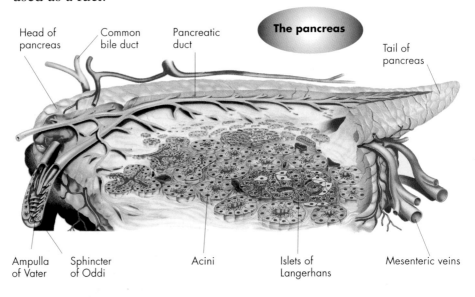

Head of pancreas   Common bile duct   Pancreatic duct   **The pancreas**   Tail of pancreas

Ampulla of Vater   Sphincter of Oddi   Acini   Islets of Langerhans   Mesenteric veins

FACT FILE

When a doctor replaces a damaged organ with a healthy one from a donor, the operation is called a transplant. Nowadays the heart, liver, kidneys and lungs can all be transplanted.

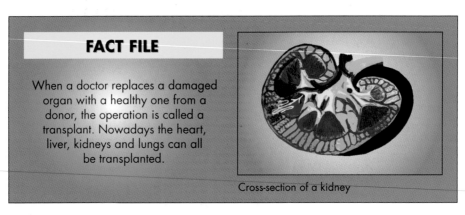

Cross-section of a kidney

WHICH PART OF THE BODY STORES BILE?

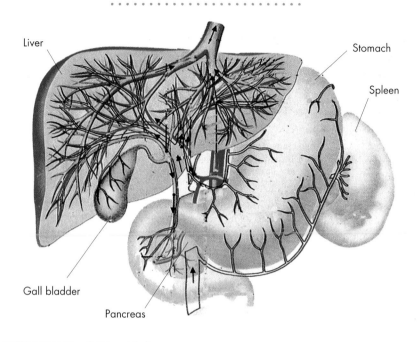

Liver

Stomach

Spleen

Gall bladder

Pancreas

FACT FILE

Sometimes the gall bladder gets filled with hard lumps, on average about the size of a pea. These are called gallstones. They are made from various substances, chiefly cholesterol and calcium and can sometimes be removed by laser surgery.

On the right underside of the liver is the gall bladder, and this small bag that contains a yellowish fluid called bile. Bile is a solution of cholesterol, bile salts and pigments. The liver makes up to a full quart of bile every day. Some of this stays in the liver and some in the gall bladder – that is until you have a meal. Then bile flows from the gall bladder and liver to a main tube, called the common bile duct, which empties into the small intestine. Bile is a waste product from the liver, but it also helps with digestion. The mineral salts in it break up, or emulsify, fatty foods in the intestine by turning the fats into tiny droplets.

WHICH BONES FORM YOUR PELVIS?

Two big, symmetrical hipbones form the pelvis. These bones join in front to form the pubic symphysis. In the back, they form a strong union with the sacrum. Each hipbone in an adult appears to be one solid bone, but it is formed by three bones, the ilium, the ischium and the pubis, that unite as the body matures. The ilium is the broad, flat bone you feel when you rest your hand on your hip. When you sit down, much of your weight rests on the ischium.

   The pelvis is the bony structure that supports the lower abdomen. It surrounds the urinary bladder, the last portion of the large intestine, and, in women, the reproductive organs. A female's pelvis is flatter and broader than a male's and it has a larger central cavity.

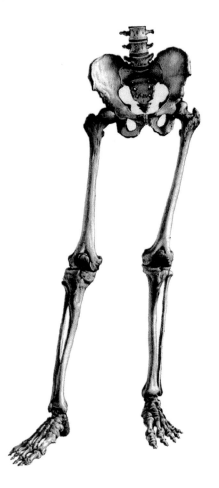

FACT FILE

The spinal column joins the pelvis at the sacroiliac joints. The femurs (thigh bones) join the lower part of the pelvis with large ball-and-socket hip joints that allow the legs to move in many directions.

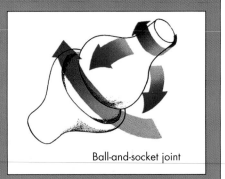

Ball-and-socket joint

IN WHICH PART OF THE BODY WOULD YOU FIND THE METACARPALS?

The metacarpals are bones in the human hand. The hand consists of the carpals (wrist bones), the metacarpals (palm bones) and the phalanges (four fingers and thumb). There are 27 bones in the hand. Eight carpal bones make up the wrist. They are arranged roughly in two rows. In the row nearest the forearm, starting from the thumb side, are the scaphoid, lunate, triquetrum and pisiform bones. In the second row are the trapezium, trapezoid, capitate and hamate bones. Five long metacarpal bones make up the palm. They connect the wrist with the fingers and thumb. Each of the four fingers contains three slender phalanges. However, the thumb contains only two phalanges.

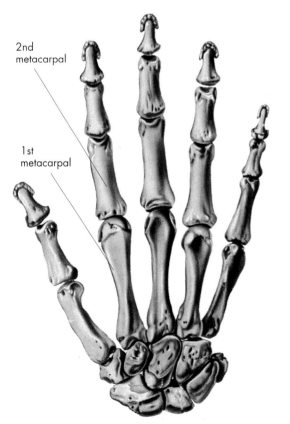

2nd metacarpal

1st metacarpal

FACT FILE

Muscles can't push, they can only pull. Muscles are pulling gently against each other most of the time. This keeps them firm and stops them from becoming floppy. Muscles get bigger and stronger if you exercise them. Muscles are joined to bones by tough 'bands' called tendons.

WHICH BONES MAKE UP THE SPINE?

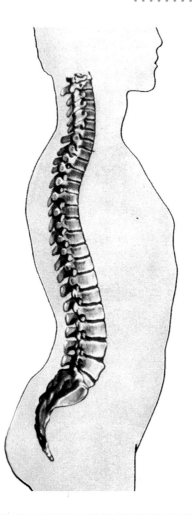

The spine is made up of a column of bones called vertebrae. The spine is the part of the skeleton that extends down the middle of the back. The spine plays an important role in posture and movement, and it also protects the spinal cord. The spine is also called the spinal column, vertebral column, or backbone. The human spine consists of 33 vertebrae, but some of them grow together in adults. There are 7 cervical (neck), 12 thoracic (chest region), 5 lumbar (lower back), 5 sacral (hip region) and 4 coccygeal (tailbone region) vertebrae. The vertebrae are held in place by muscles and strong connective tissue called ligaments. Most vertebrae have fibrous intervertebral discs between them to absorb shock and enable the spine to bend. The spine normally has a slight natural curve.

FACT FILE

Many people suffer from backaches. Sometimes the intervertebral disc, the tissue that lies between the vertebrae, sticks out and presses on nerves. This condition is called a slipped disc. It can cause severe pain in the lower back, thighs and legs.

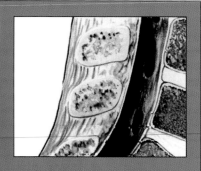

WHICH IS THE SMALLEST BONE IN YOUR BODY?

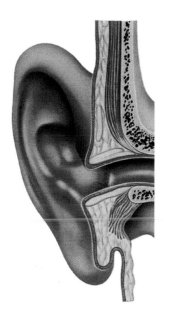

FACT FILE

Some people suffer from motion sickness when they travel by boat, car, train or aeroplane. Motion sickness is caused by excessive stimulation of the vestibular organs. But researchers do not know why some people develop motion sickness more easily than others.

The smallest bone in the body is called the stirrup. It is in the middle ear and is part of the system that carries sound signals to the brain. At only 3 mm long, the stirrup is just about the size of a grain of rice. The footplate of the stirrup bone is attached to a membrane called the oval window, which leads to the inner ear. It is connected to two other very small bones called the hammer and the anvil. All three of these bones are joined to the eardrum, where sound is collected before it is sent in the form of nerve signals to the brain.

The ear is a very important organ for keeping our sense of balance. Without a sense of balance, we could not hold our body steady, and we would stagger and fall when we tried to move.

WHICH JOINT IN YOUR BODY IS THE BIGGEST?

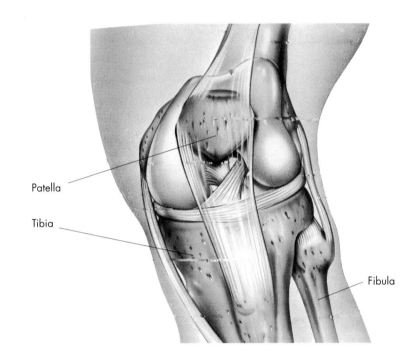

Patella

Tibia

Fibula

FACT FILE

The patella (or kneecap) is a small, flat, triangular bone in front of the joint. It is not directly connected with any other bone. Muscle attachments hold the patella in place.

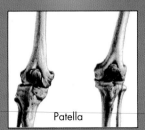

Patella

The knee joint is the largest joint in the body. It is also the most complex. The knee is the joint where the thighbone meets the large bone of the lower leg. The knee moves like a hinge, but it can also rotate and move a little from side to side. The knee is more likely to be damaged than most other joints because it is subject to tremendous forces during vigorous activity. Most of the knee injuries that occur in football and other sports result from twisting the joint. The knee ligaments are the strongest connections between the femur and the tibia. Ligaments keep the bones from moving out of position.

WHICH PART OF YOUR BODY CONTROLS BALANCE?

The inner ear is the body's main organ of balance, but the brain also receives messages from nerve-endings in the neck, back, leg and feet muscles. The brain sifts all this information and sends messages back to the muscles, allowing us to perform incredible feats of balance such as ice-skating or gymnastics. Near the cochlea are fluid-filled tubes – the semicircular canals. As your head moves about, the fluid inside each canal swishes to and fro. When the body moves, the fluid causes hairs in a jelly-like mass to bend. These are connected to the vestibular nerve, which alerts the brain to re-balance the body.

FACT FILE

You feel dizzy after you spin around because the liquid in your ears is still swirling about when you stop, and your brain can't tell where you're going! If you watch a dancer spin round, you will see that their head does not move continuously.

TELL ME WHICH : THE HUMAN BODY

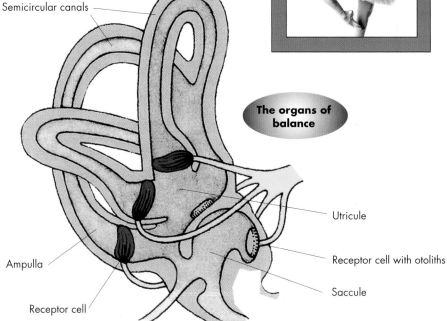

Semicircular canals

The organs of balance

Utricule

Receptor cell with otoliths

Ampulla

Saccule

Receptor cell

WHICH PART OF THE BODY HAS FOLLICLES?

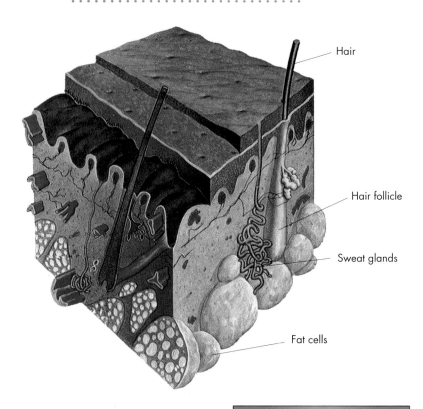

Hair

Hair follicle

Sweat glands

Fat cells

You would find a follicle at the root of an individual hair. A follicle is a long tunnel that reaches into the lower layers of the skin. At the end of the tiny tunnel, there is a hair papilla. The papilla is where most of the growth takes place, as it is here that nutrients are taken up from the blood. Slightly below the surface of the skin there are sebaceous glands which supply the hair with sufficient sebum, the fatty secretion of these glands. A tiny hair-raising muscle is responsible for providing sebum from the sebaceous glands.

FACT FILE

A nail has three parts, the matrix, the plate and the bed. The matrix lies under the surface of the skin at the base of the nail. Most of the matrix is covered by skin.

WHICH PART OF THE EYE LETS IN LIGHT?

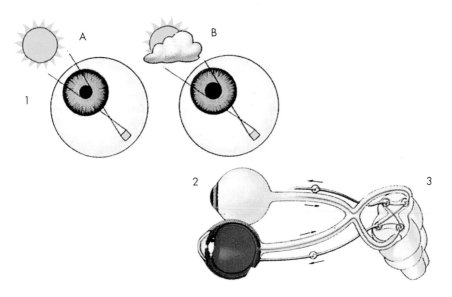

The muscles of the eye contract to make the pupil smaller in bright conditions and larger when it is dark. This controls how much light gets into the eye. Too much, and you risk damaging its delicate inner parts. The retina is very sensitive to light. Too much light (A) distorts what we see and is dazzling. The pupils vary in size and thus reduce or increase the amount of light entering the eye. Bright light causes a reflex nervous reaction, controlled by areas in the midbrain. The circular pupillary muscle (1) in both irises contracts and the radial strands (2) extend, thus narrowing the diameter. Poor light (B) will make both pupils dilate, allowing sufficient light to stimulate the cells in the retina (3).

FACT FILE

Did you know that the human eye is so sensitive that a person sitting on top of a hill on a moonless night could see a match being struck up to 80 km (50 miles) away.

IN WHICH PART OF THE BODY IS THE MANDIBLE?

In addition to 12 other bones in the face are the two that make up the jaw. These are the maxillae (upper jaw) and the mandible (lower jaw). Each contains sockets for the teeth, which are embedded in fibrous tissue. Teeth are hard, bonelike structures in the upper and lower jaws of human beings and many kinds of animals. They are the hardest parts of the body. Muscles in the head are important to the processes of chewing and swallowing. They are responsible for facial expressions, such as smiling or frowning. A system of muscles and tendons connects the head to the spinal column, the collarbone and the shoulder blades. These muscles and tendons control the movement of the head.

FACT FILE

The mandible is the only bony part of the face that moves. There are 32 permanent teeth, 16 in the mandible and 16 in the maxillae. Each jaw has 4 incisors, 2 canines, 4 premolars and 6 molars.

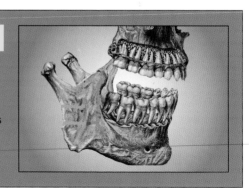

WHICH CORDS HELP YOU TO SPEAK?

The main sound producers in human beings are called vocal cords. These two small folds of tissue stretch across the larynx. The larynx is a section of the air passage in the throat. It is located between the back of the tongue and the trachea (windpipe). The larynx is sometimes called the voice box, because it contains the

vocal cords. Muscles in the larynx stretch and relax the vocal cords. When we breathe, we relax our vocal cords so they form a V-shaped opening that lets air through. When we speak, we pull the vocal cords by the attached muscles, narrowing the opening. Then, as we drive air from the lungs through the larynx, the air vibrates the tightened vocal cords and sound results. The more the cords are stretched, the higher are the sounds produced. The more relaxed the cords, the lower the sounds.

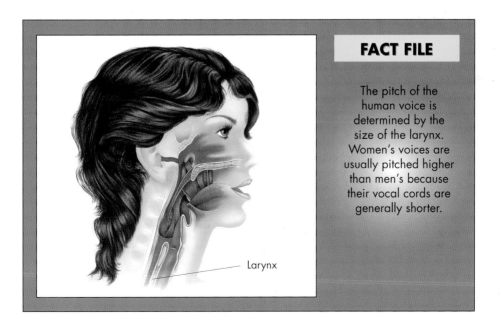

Larynx

FACT FILE

The pitch of the human voice is determined by the size of the larynx. Women's voices are usually pitched higher than men's because their vocal cords are generally shorter.

WHICH BUDS COAT YOUR TONGUE?

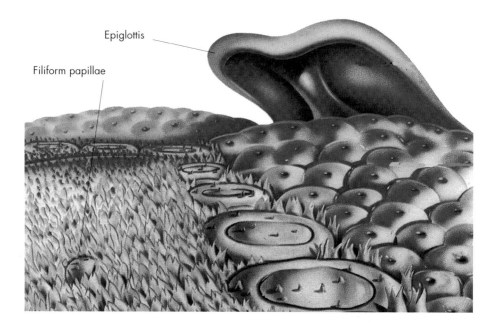

Epiglottis

Filiform papillae

Papillae are found on the surface of your tongue – you probably know them as taste buds. The chief organ of taste, the tongue also helps in chewing and swallowing, and plays an important part in forming the sounds of words. Covered with a mucous membrane, the undersurface of the tongue is smooth, but many papillae give the top of the tongue a rough surface.

There are four kinds of papillae: filiform, folioform and vallate – found only at the back of the tongue – and fungiform. These four types of taste buds enable us to distinguish between the sweet, sour, salty and bitter tastes in things we eat.

FACT FILE

The sense of taste is the crudest of our five senses. It is limited in both range and versatility. Each papilla contains one to two hundred taste buds.

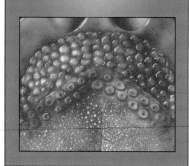

IN WHICH PART OF THE BODY DOES DIGESTION START?

Digestion starts in the mouth. Chewing is very important for good digestion for two reasons. When chewed food is ground into fine particles, the digestive juices can act more easily. As the food is chewed, it is moistened and mixed with saliva, which contains the enzyme ptyalin. Ptyalin changes some of the starches

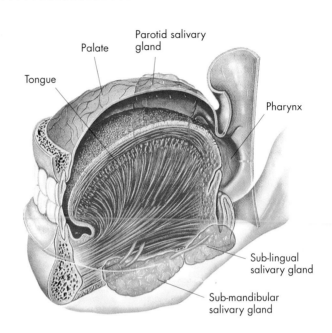

Palate

Parotid salivary gland

Tongue

Pharynx

Sub-lingual salivary gland

Sub-mandibular salivary gland

in the food to sugar. After the food is swallowed, it passes through the oesophagus into the stomach. The digestive juice in the stomach is called gastric juice. It contains hydrochloric acid and the enzyme pepsin. This juice begins the digestion of protein foods such as meat, eggs and milk. Starches, sugars and fats are not digested by the gastric juice. After a meal, some food remains in the stomach for two to five hours.

FACT FILE

Almost no digestion occurs in the large intestine. The large intestine stores waste food products and absorbs water and small amounts of minerals. The waste materials that accumulate in the large intestine are roughage that cannot be digested in the body.

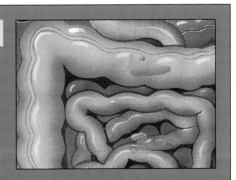

IN WHICH PART OF THE BODY DOES DIGESTION END?

In the small intestine, the digestive process is completed on the partly digested food by pancreatic juice, intestinal juice and bile. The pancreatic juice is produced by the pancreas and pours into the small intestine through a tube, or duct. The intestinal juice is produced by the walls of the small intestine. It has milder digestive effects than pancreatic juice but carries out a similar digestion. Bile is produced in the liver, stored in the gallbladder, and flows into the small intestine through the bile duct. When the food is completely digested, it is absorbed by tiny blood and lymph vessels in the walls of the small intestine. It is then carried into the circulation for nourishment of the body. Food particles are small enough to pass through the walls of the intestine and blood vessels only when they are completely digested.

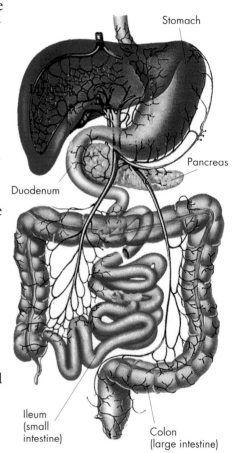

Stomach

Liver

Pancreas

Duodenum

Ileum (small intestine)

Colon (large intestine)

FACT FILE

The small intestine is about 7 m (23 ft) long and is lined with small finger-like protuberances called villi. The successful absorption of nutrients depends on their transport away from the cells of the villi into the bloodstream.

IN WHICH PART OF THE BODY IS THE ACHILLES TENDON?

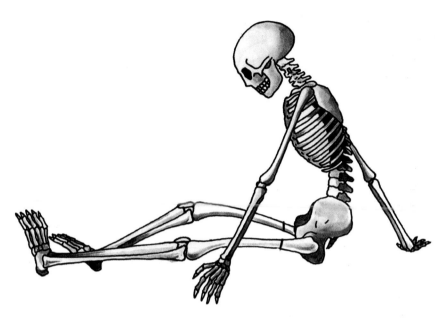

You'll find it at the back of the ankle. A tendon, also called a sinew, is a strong white cord that attaches muscles to bones and we have them all over our bodies. The Achilles attaches the muscles of the calf to the heel bone and is one of the strongest tendons in the body. The name Achilles tendon comes from the legend of Achilles, a Greek hero killed by an arrow in the heel. The Achilles tendon may rupture as the result of a powerful upward movement of the foot or a blow to the calf when the calf muscles are contracted. This injury most commonly occurs in people over the age of 30 who compete in sports that involve running.

FACT FILE

Thirty-five powerful muscles move the human hand. Fifteen are in the forearm rather than in the hand itself. This arrangement gives great strength to the hand without making the fingers so thick with muscles that they would be difficult to move.

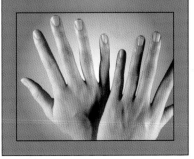

WHICH PART OF THE BODY STORES URINE?

The bladder is the common name for the urinary bladder, a hollow muscular organ that stores urine before expelling it from the body. The emptying of the urinary bladder is voluntarily controlled in most human beings and many other mammals. The bladder lies just behind the pubis, one of the bones of the pelvis.

Urine drains continuously from the kidneys into the bladder through two tubes called ureters. It leaves the bladder through the urethra, a wider tube that leads out of the body. The place where the bladder and the urethra meet is called the neck of the bladder. A complex arrangement of muscles encircles the bladder neck. This ring, called the urethral sphincter, normally prevents urine from leaving the bladder.

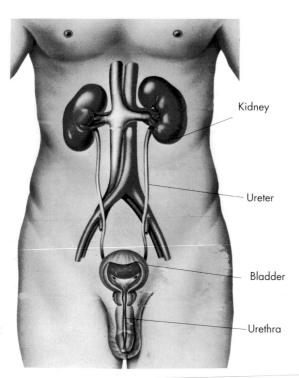

Kidney

Ureter

Bladder

Urethra

The bladder can hold more than ½ l (1 pt) of urine.

FACT FILE

We lose around 3 l (5 pt) of water a day through our skin as sweat, and in our breath and urine. We also get rid of extra salt in sweat and we expel waste carbon dioxide gas when we breathe out.

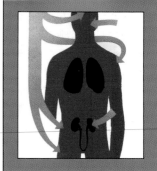

WHICH CELLS ARE MADE IN BONE MARROW?

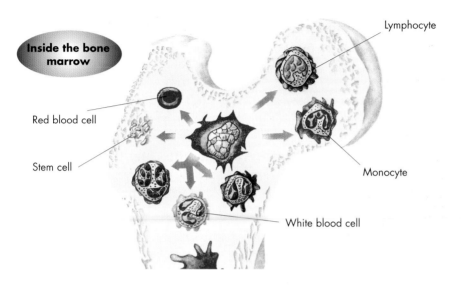

Inside the bone marrow

Lymphocyte

Red blood cell

Stem cell

Monocyte

White blood cell

Both white and red blood cells are formed in bone marrow. Each red blood cell measure about 7.5 microns (thousandths of a millimetre) in diameter and are shaped a little like doughnuts. They contain haemoglobin, which gives their red pigment. There are 5 to 6 million red cells per cubic mm of blood. The red cell only survives about 120 days and the damaged and old cells are removed by the spleen and the liver. A white blood cell is not really white but almost transparent. It can change shape, push out folds and finger-like projections and move along by oozing and crawling like an amoeba in a pond. These cells survive less than a week.

FACT FILE

An average adult has about 5 l (8 pt) of blood. At any one time, about 1,250 ml (1½ pt) are in the arteries, 3,500 ml (6 pt) in the veins and about 250 ml (½ pt) in the capillaries. The cells in blood flow through a capillary for only half a second before they move into the next type of vessels, veins.

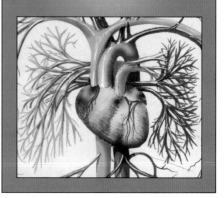

IN WHICH PART OF THE BODY DOES SPERM DEVELOP?

Sperm, the male sex cells, develop in the testes. It is stored for several days until needed. The testes contain long tubes called the seminiferous tubules, which are tightly coiled. Sperm is produced continuously in these tubes, then passed to the epididymis and stored in a large duct called the vas deferens. Here liquid is added to the sperm to make a milky fluid called semen. It is stored in pouches called seminal vesicles. During sexual intercourse the seminal vesicles contract and force out the sperm.

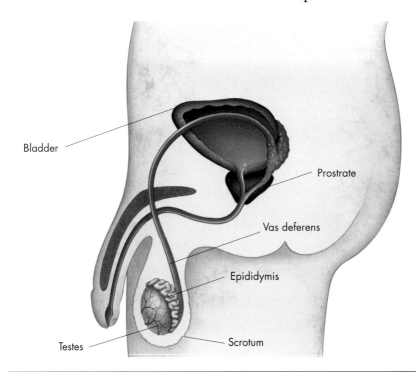

Bladder

Prostrate

Vas deferens

Epididymis

Testes

Scrotum

FACT FILE

Up to 100 million sperms are produced every day by the male. If they are not released they are soon destroyed and replaced. Sperms look like tiny tadpoles with rounded heads and long lashing tails.

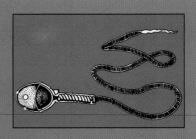

WHICH PROCESS ENDS IN MENSTRUATION?

Menstruation, also known as a period, is the loss of blood and cells that occurs about once a month in most women of child-bearing age. It takes place through the vagina. During each month, blood and cells build up in the lining of a woman's uterus (or womb), a hollow, pear-shaped organ that holds a baby during pregnancy. The thickening of the lining prepares the uterus for pregnancy. If pregnancy does not occur, the lining breaks down. The blood and cells are discharged through the vagina, which is a canal that leads from the uterus to the outside of the body. The process of menstruation lasts from three to seven days, and this period of time is called the menstrual period.

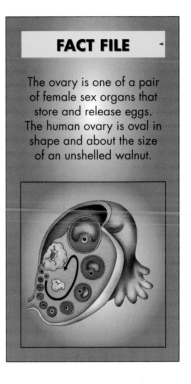

FACT FILE

The ovary is one of a pair of female sex organs that store and release eggs. The human ovary is oval in shape and about the size of an unshelled walnut.

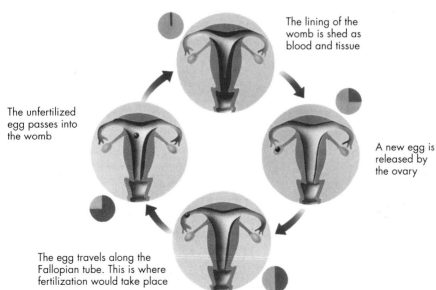

The lining of the womb is shed as blood and tissue

A new egg is released by the ovary

The egg travels along the Fallopian tube. This is where fertilization would take place

The unfertilized egg passes into the womb

THE
SOLAR
SYSTEM

CONTENTS

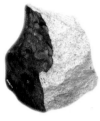

THROUGH WHICH PROCESS DID THE UNIVERSE BEGIN? 180
WHICH ELEMENTS MAKE UP THE UNIVERSE? 181

WHICH IS THE BRIGHTEST STAR IN THE SOLAR SYSTEM? 182
WHICH IS THE PROCESS THAT CREATES SUNSHINE? 183

WHICH PLANET IS CLOSEST TO THE SUN? 184
WHICH GALAXY IS EARTH IN? 185

WHICH PLANET IS THE HOTTEST? 186
WHICH PLANET IS CALLED THE RED PLANET? 187

WHICH IS MARS'S LARGEST VOLCANO? 188
WHICH PLANET IS THE BIGGEST? 189

WHICH OF THE PLANETS HAVE RINGS? 190
WHICH BELT IS FOUND IN SPACE? 191

WHICH PLANET IS ALWAYS DARK AND COLD? 192
WHICH PLANET HAS THE MOST MOONS? 193

WHICH MOON IS BIGGER THAN PLUTO? 194
WHICH SPACE OBJECTS ARE THE DARKEST? 195

WHICH CLOUDS LIE FAR OUT IN SPACE? 196
WHICH WIND BLOWS IN SPACE? 197

WHICH SPACE PROBE WAS THE FIRST TO LAUNCH? 198
WHICH SPACE OBJECTS HAVE TAILS? 199

WHICH COMET IS THE MOST FAMOUS? 200
WHICH EARTHBOUND METEORITE WAS THE LARGEST? 201

WHICH PROCESS CREATES A SUPERNOVA? 202
WHICH PHENOMENON IS KNOWN AS A NEBULA? 203

WHICH ARE THE THREE MAIN TYPES OF METEORITE? 204
WHICH ASTEROID IS THE BIGGEST? 205

WHICH NATION LAUNCHED THE FIRST SPACE SHUTTLE? 206
WHICH NATIONS HAVE SPACE STATIONS? 207

THROUGH WHICH PROCESS DID THE UNIVERSE BEGIN?

Nobody knows how the Universe began, but the most common theory is the Big Bang. According to this theory, the Universe was formed from an immense explosion 13 billion years ago. Before the Big Bang, everything in the Universe was packed into a tiny area, smaller than the nucleus of an atom. This point was called a singularity and was incredibly hot. It was released in an explosion so powerful that all of the matter in the singularity was blasted into an area larger than a galaxy in less than a fraction of a second. There is very strong evidence to support the theory of the Big Bang. The strongest 'proof' is a weak signal that has been detected in space. This is thought to be an echo from the energy released by the force of the Big Bang.

FACT FILE

According to ancient Egyptian mythology, the fundamentals of life – air (Shu) and moisture (Tefnut) – came from the spittle of their Sun God Re. From the union of Shu and Tefnut came Geb, the Earth god, and Nut, the sky goddess. The first human beings were born from Re's tears.

WHICH ELEMENTS MAKE UP THE UNIVERSE?

The Universe is everything and anything that exists. The Universe is still a mystery to scientists. The Universe is made up almost entirely of hydrogen and helium. These are the two lightest elements. All the rest of the matter in the Universe is very rare. Elements such as silicon, carbon and others are concentrated into clouds, stars and planets. The Universe is held together by four invisible forces. Gravity and electromagnetism are the two familiar forces. The other two kinds are strong and weak nuclear forces. These operate only inside the incredibly tiny nuclei of atoms, holding the tiny particles together.

FACT FILE

The large Hadron Collider, successfully tested in 2010 will teach us more about particle acceleration and the birth of stars and the deepest laws of nature.

WHICH IS THE BRIGHTEST STAR IN THE SOLAR SYSTEM?

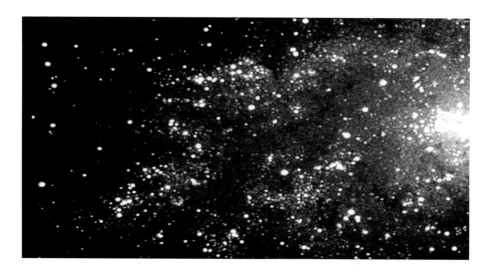

The brightest star in the solar system is the Sun. A star is a giant ball of glowing gas in space fuelled by nuclear reactions in its core. You can see several thousand stars with the naked eye. But these are only the brightest stars. Astronomers have found tens of millions more stars by using powerful telescopes to probe the sky. Our star, the Sun, is an ordinary star. Compared to the Sun, some stars are giants. They each contain enough matter to make tens or hundreds of Suns. A star's brightness depends on how bright it really is, it's size, how hot it is and how far away. The closer a star is to Earth, and the larger it is, the brighter it looks.

FACT FILE

Most stars are not single stars like the Sun. They have at least one companion star and the two stars orbit each other. Some pairs of stars look close together only because they lie in the same direction from Earth, but their movements show that they are not orbiting each other.

WHICH IS THE PROCESS THAT CREATES SUNSHINE?

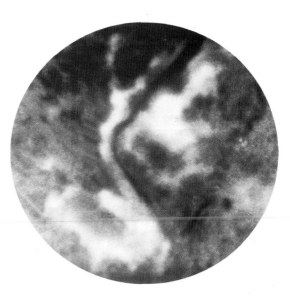

Our Sun is a star and, like in most other stars, it shines because of a process called nuclear fusion that is taking place at its core: atoms of hydrogen collide and are combined into atoms of helium at very high temperatures and pressures. In the formation of the helium atoms tiny amounts of mass are lost and converted into a huge amount of energy. Over millions of years, this energy makes its way out from the core of the Sun and eventually reaches the Sun's surface where it is emitted as light, heat, ultraviolet radiation and X-rays. From the surface of the Sun, it takes about eight minutes for the light and other radiation to reach the Earth. Fusion started in the Sun about five billion years ago and, although 600 billion kg (1,320 lb) of hydrogen is being converted to helium every singles second, it will continue to do so for about the same length of time.

FACT FILE

As stars go, our Sun is very small. It is of a type known as a yellow dwarf. The colour of a star shows its surface temperature: red stars are relatively cool, while blue stars are hotter.

WHICH PLANET IS CLOSEST TO THE SUN?

Known by most ancient people from its brief periods of visibility at dawn and dusk, Mercury is the closest planet to the Sun. The planet was named after the Roman winged messenger of the gods – because it has the fastest orbital speed of any planet, averaging 47 km (29 miles) every second. Being the closest planet to the Sun, it is blasted by solar heat and other radiation. This has swept away all but the flimsiest atmosphere, and heats Mercury's daytime side to incredible temperatures – yet the night side plunges to within 100°C (148°F) of absolute zero. Between 2011 and 2013, NASA's Messenger spacecraft mapped the entire planet for the first time in history. The planet has several hundred named craters, with names like Dickens, Shakespeare, Chopin, Mark Twain, Beethoven, Degas and Sibelius – all named after famous artists and classical musicians. Among the planet's features are the Caloris Montes, or 'Hot Mountains' – curved ranges with peaks rising to 3,000 m (9,840 ft) sited at one of the hottest places on Mercury, within the Caloris Basin crater and Discovery Scarp. Joining two craters, this 'cliff' is 350 km (220 miles) long and its maximum height is around 2,800 m (9,185 ft).

FACT FILE

Perhaps the best-known feature on Mercury is the Caloris Basin – a massive crater measuring 1,350 km (840 miles) across made by asteroid/meteoroid impact.

WHICH GALAXY IS EARTH IN?

FACT FILE

There are at least 300 billion stars in the galaxy. And here is an idea of its size. It takes eight minutes for light from the Sun to reach the Earth. For light from the middle of the galaxy to reach the Sun, it takes about 27,000 years.

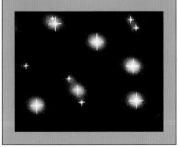

Our Solar System is part of a galaxy that we call the Milky Way. If you could get above it and look down on it, it would look like an immense watchface. But we are inside the galaxy, and when we look up we are looking towards the edge from inside the 'watch'. So we see that edge curving around us. As there are millions of stars in it, we see it as the Milky Way. There is probably nothing more mysterious and wonderful-looking in the sky than the Milky Way, stretching like a band of jewels from one end of the sky to the other. In early Christian times people thought it was a pathway for the angels, so they could go up to heaven on it. But today we know the real facts about the Milky Way.

185

WHICH PLANET IS THE HOTTEST?

The hottest planet in the Solar System is Venus, the second closest planet to the Sun. Venus is named after the Roman goddess of love – and is shrouded in mystery. In fact, it is shrouded by thick swirling clouds of gases and droplets of acid that hide its surface from the gaze of outsiders. Although Venus is about the same size and mass ('weight') as Earth, it could not be more different. It is the hottest of all the planets, partly because its thick atmosphere traps vast amounts of heat from the nearby Sun. Several probes have been sent to Venus, and radio waves have been used to map virtually the entire planet. Among its major features are the Ishtar Terra to the north. These highlands are about the size of Australia and bear Venus's highest mountains. Other features include Arachnoid volcanoes, which have unusual ridges around them. The central volcano with its surrounding ridges looks like a giant spider. All of Venus's surface features are named after females (either real people or from myth and legend), with the exception of the Maxwell Montes, named after scientist James Clerk Maxwell.

FACT FILE

The surface of Venus is hard and rocky, with numerous volcanoes, including Sif Mons, pictured here. It was photographed by the Magellan space probe.

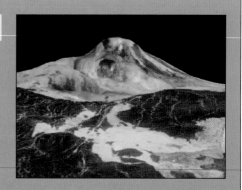

WHICH PLANET IS CALLED THE RED PLANET?

Named after the Roman god of war, Mars is also called the 'Red Planet' because its surface rocks and dust contain large amounts of the substance iron oxide – better known here on Earth as rust. Mars shares many features with Earth, including volcanoes, canyons, winds and swirling dust storms. Among its landmark features is Olympus Mons, the largest volcano in solar system. At nearly 24 km (15 miles) high – three times the height Mount Everest. Features resembling riverbeds, estuaries and shorelines suggest that great rivers – probably of water – once flowed across Mars' surface. Despite many visits by space probes, landers and rovers, no signs of life have ever been found.

Humans have always toyed with the idea that Martians inhabit the Red Planet, most famously in H G Wells *War of the Worlds* (1898), which featured a Martian invasion of Earth.

FACT FILE

Like Earth, Mars has polar ice caps made of water ice that remains through summer.

January 2001

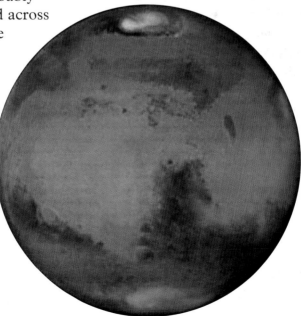

WHICH IS MARS'S LARGEST VOLCANO?

Mars has one of the most striking surfaces of any planet in the Solar System. Giant volcanoes tower above the landscape. The largest of these is Olympus Mons, which is 25 km (15.5 miles) tall, three times larger than Mount Everest. As well as this, Mars is home to Valles Marineris, a canyon that is 180 km (112 miles) wide, up to 7 km (4.3 miles) deep and long enough to stretch across America.

Mars does not have water on its surface now, but there is evidence to show that there were rivers and seas on Mars in the past. Probes have taken many pictures of the planet's surface and scientists have identified several channels that could only have been formed by running water. Astronomers believe that there was a great deal of liquid on Mars billions of years ago.

FACT FILE

In 1996 scientists produced evidence they claimed, that showed living creatures inhabited Mars more than 3.6 billion years ago.

WHICH PLANET IS THE BIGGEST?

By far the biggest planet in the Solar System is Jupiter – a vast world of swirling gases and storms of unimaginable fury. It is the fifth planet from the Sun in terms of distance, but is also, the nearest 'gas giant' to the Sun. It has more than twice as much mass ('weight') than all the other eight planets added together. Jupiter is not much smaller than some of the stars called brown dwarfs, but it does not shine itself, and reflects sunlight as all planets do. Even so, its huge pull of gravity holds more than 60 moons in orbit around it. Of its moons, Ganymede is the largest in the Solar System, Callisto is the most heavily cratered object and Io probably has the most volcanic activity. Jupiter is named after the Roman king of the gods, also called Jove. Jupiter is not only the largest planet, it also spins around the fastest, once in less than 10 Earth hours. The spinning speed of the upper atmosphere at the equator is 5 minutes faster than at the poles, so the atmosphere is continually being twisted and torn.

FACT FILE

Jupiter has several distinctive features mapped by astronomers. The best known is the Great Red Spot, a giant storm system three times wider than Earth. It travels around Jupiter just south of the equator, once every six days.

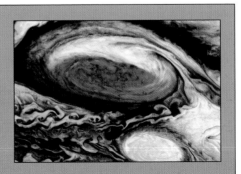

WHICH OF THE PLANETS HAVE RINGS?

Saturn, the second-largest planet after neighbouring Jupiter is perhaps the best-known planet for having rings. They are made of billions of fragments of ice and rock, which reflect sunlight and so glisten and sparkle. The largest particles are car-sized. Due to its fast spin, 'gas giant' make-up and very light weight compared to its size, Saturn bulges around its middle, or equator, as it rotates. This means the planet is fatter than it is tall by almost 12,000 km (7,450 miles). Saturn is the only planet whose density, or mass per volume, is less than water. We would say it is 'lighter than water' and if there was a tank of water big enough to run a bath for this enormous planet, Saturn would float in it!

Although Saturn is the planet everyone thinks of when it comes to having rings, the three remaining gas giants – Jupiter, Neptune and Uranus have ring systems, too.

FACT FILE

The rings of Saturn were first noticed by Galileo, who could not quite make them out with his early telescope. He guessed they might be moons, one on each side, and called them 'ears of Saturn'.

WHICH BELT IS FOUND IN SPACE?

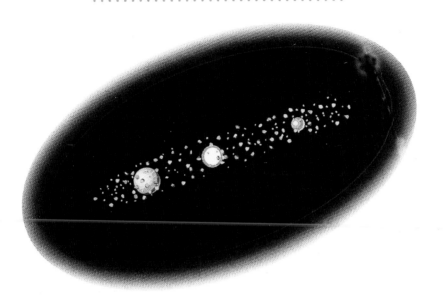

FACT FILE

An object in space will be pulled into a spherical shape if its gravitational force is powerful enough. Because the objects in the Kuiper Belt do not have powerful gravitational pulls, they come in all sorts of shapes and sizes.

The Kuiper belt is found in space and lies way beyond the planet Neptune. It was named after the astronomer, Gerard Kuiper who suggested that the belt was full of celestial bodies made up from rock and ice. Astronomers now think that there may be as many as 100,000 large, comet-like objects in this region and that they include the planet Pluto. The icy bodies in the Kuiper Belt are called minor members, or 'Plutinos' because they act like little Plutos and are very difficult to spot from Earth, even with the most powerful telescopes. If all the objects in the Kuiper Belt joined together, they would form a planet the size of Earth.

WHICH PLANET IS ALWAYS DARK AND COLD?

It is always dark and cold on Pluto, even in the middle of the day. This is because the Sun appears 1,000 times fainter from the surface of Pluto than it does from Earth, little more than a faint star. In summer, Pluto has a slight atmosphere because the surface warms up enough to melt some of its ice, turning it to gas. As Pluto moves away from the Sun, the gas freezes and becomes ices again. This means that in winter, Pluto's weather doesn't just become worse, it completely disappears.

FACT FILE

Little is known about Pluto's atmosphere, but it probably consists primarily of nitrogen with some carbon monoxide and methane.

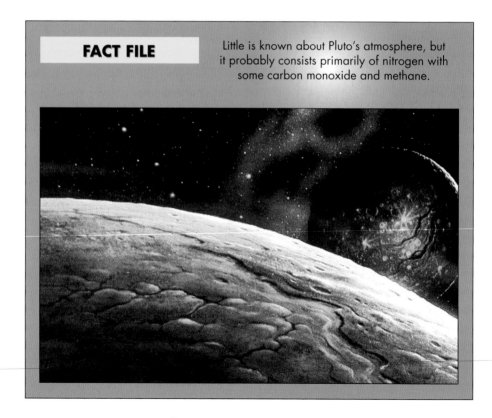

WHICH PLANET HAS THE MOST MOONS?

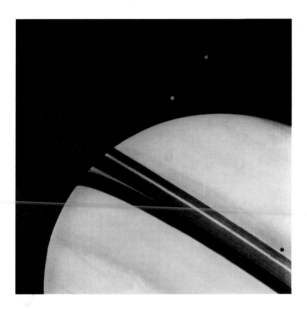

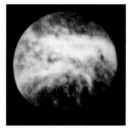

Ganymede

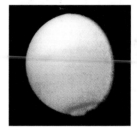

Titan

A moon is any natural satellite orbiting a planet. All the planets in our Universe have moons with the exception of Mercury and Venus. Earth only has one moon and that is the Moon itself, which takes a total of 27.3 days to orbit our planet. Pluto also only has one moon. It is called Charon. Next comes Mars which has two moons called Phobos and Deimos. Neptune has eight moons. Uranus has 15 moons. Next is Jupiter with 16 moons. Finally, the planet with the most moons is Saturn, which has 18 moons with orbiting times of 0.57 to 550.4 days.

FACT FILE

Io is one of the moons that orbits Jupiter. Its diameter is 3,640 km (2,260 miles), it is 421,800 km (262,000 miles) from Jupiter and takes a total of 0.7 Earth days to orbit the planet.

WHICH MOON IS BIGGER THAN PLUTO?

Callisto is a moon of Jupiter, and it is bigger than the dwarf planet Pluto and almost as large as Mercury. It is one of the most heavily cratered bodies in the Solar System. Its surface is covered with craters of all sizes caused by the impact of asteroids and comets. More than four billion years of bombardment have darkened Callisto's icy surface. The biggest impacts cracked the surface to form huge bull's-eye patterns. The surface is blanketed by dark dirt that accumulated when icy crater rims and cliffs crumbled away. This satellite has a carbon dioxide atmosphere that is only slightly denser than the near-vacuum of outer space.

FACT FILE

Callisto has a diameter of 4,806 km (2,986 miles). It orbits Jupiter every 16.7 days at a distance of 1,883,000 km (1,170,000 miles). The Italian astronomer Galileo discovered Callisto in 1610.

WHICH SPACE OBJECTS ARE THE DARKEST?

The darkest objects in space are black holes – the monsters of the Universe. Formed from the brightest of all explosions, supernovae, they soon become the darkest objects in space, emitting no light at all. A black hole is an area in space where the force of gravity is so strong that even light cannot escape from it. Black holes are created when a burned-out star collapses. Eventually it shrinks into a tiny sphere of material. The gravity of this material is so powerful that it pulls in everything around it. Even light itself is sucked into the black hole. Nothing that goes into a black hole ever comes out. We cannot see black holes. We can sometimes identify them from the radio waves given off as a star is drawn into a black hole.

FACT FILE

Imagine space as a stretched-out sheet. If an object is placed on this sheet, it will create a dip, towards which other objects will be drawn if they come too close. A black hole creates such a steep dip that objects that enter can never escape.

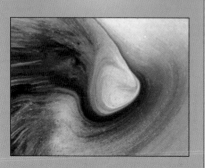

WHICH CLOUDS LIE FAR OUT IN SPACE?

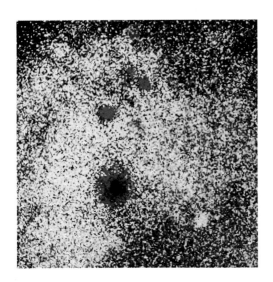

Two galaxies visible in the southern hemisphere as small, hazy patches of light are referred to as the Magellanic Clouds. They are the galaxies closest to the Milky Way, the galaxy that contains the Sun, the Earth and the rest of our Solar System. Astronomers classify the Magellanic Clouds as irregular galaxies because the distribution of the stars within them does not follow a particular pattern. The Magellanic Clouds contain billions of stars, but individual stars can be distinguished only by using the most powerful telescopes. As a result, the galaxies appear cloudy to the naked eye. The Magellanic Clouds also contain a huge quantity of gas. New stars are constantly forming from this gas, which is composed mainly of hydrogen. In addition, much of the light from the Magellanic Clouds comes from young, extremely luminous, hot blue stars that are surrounded by glowing clouds of this gas.

FACT FILE

Magellanic Clouds were first recorded in the early 16th century during the world's first circumnavigation by the Portuguese explorer Ferdinand Magellan, after whom they were named.

WHICH WIND BLOWS IN SPACE?

Charged particles are constantly being given off by the Sun. They are known as the solar wind and are strongest when the sunspot activity is at its height. When the solar wind reaches the Earth's magnetic field, the charged particles interact with gases in the Earth's atmosphere 10 km (6 miles) above the surface. This interaction causes the particles to send out light, which is seen from Earth as an amazing light show, best visible from within the Arctic and Antarctic Circles. In the northern hemisphere this is known as the aurora borealis, and in the southern hemisphere as the aurora australis.

FACT FILE

Darker areas on the surface of the Sun are called sunspots. These areas of cooler gas occur when the Sun's magnetic field blocks the flow of heat from the core.

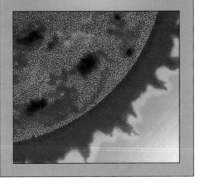

WHICH SPACE PROBE WAS THE FIRST TO LAUNCH?

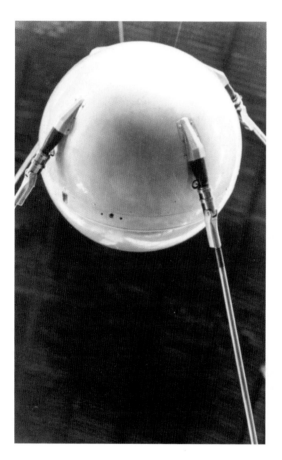

Unmanned space probes have toured almost the entire Solar System. The first probes were blasted into space towards the end of the 1950s when the Cold War between the United States and the Soviet Union was at its height. The world's first artificial satellite was Sputnik 1 on 4 Oct 1957. Since that time probes have explored the surface of Mars, created maps of Venus and Mercury, taken close-up photographs of nearly all the planets and many of their moons, orbited Saturn and even left the Solar System altogether.

FACT FILE

Laika the dog was the first-ever space traveller. A stray dog from the streets of Moscow, Laika was one of three dogs trained for the mission. Her big day came when she was selected to enter space aboard the Soviet spacecraft Sputnik 2 on 2 November 1957.

WHICH SPACE OBJECTS HAVE TAILS?

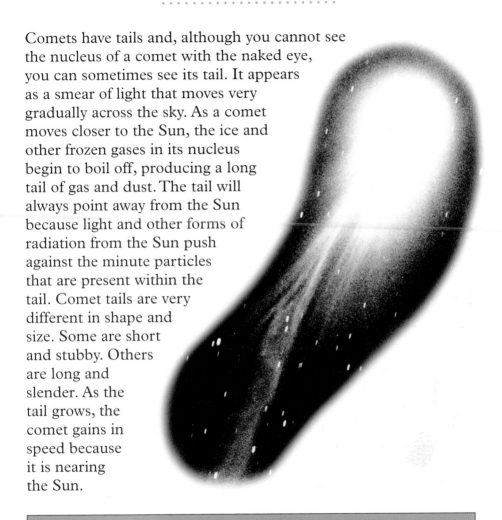

Comets have tails and, although you cannot see the nucleus of a comet with the naked eye, you can sometimes see its tail. It appears as a smear of light that moves very gradually across the sky. As a comet moves closer to the Sun, the ice and other frozen gases in its nucleus begin to boil off, producing a long tail of gas and dust. The tail will always point away from the Sun because light and other forms of radiation from the Sun push against the minute particles that are present within the tail. Comet tails are very different in shape and size. Some are short and stubby. Others are long and slender. As the tail grows, the comet gains in speed because it is nearing the Sun.

FACT FILE

Halley's Comet is perhaps the most famous comet of all. It can be seen from Earth every 76 years and was even recorded in 1066 on the Bayeux Tapestry.

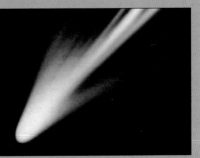

WHICH COMET IS THE MOST FAMOUS?

Every few years, an object that looks like a fuzzy star with a long bright tail appears in the sky. These strange objects are not stars. They are comets. A comet is a chunk of gas and dust and ice left over from the formation of the Solar System.

Comets orbit the Sun. When a comet nears the Sun, some of the ice on its surface evaporates and releases dust to form a tail. Most comets are too dim to be seen with the naked eye, but every 10 years or so an especially bright comet appears in the sky. About 850 comets have been spotted and listed by astronomers and perhaps the most famous is Halley's comet, which reappears every 76 years. It is named after the astronomer Edmond Halley. It even appears in the Bayeux Tapestry that records the Battle of Hastings of 1066.

FACT FILE

Most comets orbit the Sun so far away that they cannot be seen. Halley's comet has an elongated orbit, which means it takes a long time to go around the Sun.

WHICH EARTHBOUND METEORITE WAS THE LARGEST?

Meteorites are made of rock or metal. They enter the Earth's atmosphere at speeds of at least 11 km (6.8 miles) per second, which makes them glow brightly. Several thousand meteorites enter the Earth's atmosphere every year, but very few of them reach the ground. The largest known meteorite is made of iron and weighs 66 tonnes (73 tons). It probably fell to the Earth in prehistoric times in what is now called Namibia, southwest Africa. Recently, researchers have been finding meteorites on the ice sheets in the Arctic and the Antarctic, where they are easier to locate.

On planets and moons with no atmosphere, huge numbers of meteorites strike with enormous power. Our own Moon is estimated to have 3,000,000 meteorite craters measuring 1 m (3 ft) or more in diameter.

FACT FILE

An enormous meteorite caused this huge impact crater at Wolf Creek in Australia. The amount of energy the impact released would have been equivalent to hundreds of nuclear weapons.

WHICH PROCESS CREATES A SUPERNOVA?

A supernova takes place when a star collapses as it begins to burn out, then suddenly explodes, producing a huge amount of light energy, and leaving behind a tiny core of neutrons, which is the heaviest substance in the Universe. Sometimes a star appears in the sky quite suddenly.

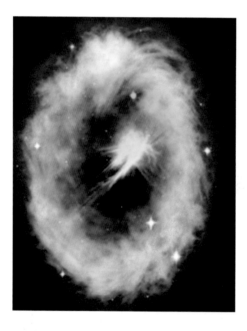

This happens when there is a pair of stars rotating together. These are called binaries, and there is usually one large star called a red giant, orbiting with a smaller, hotter star. The nova takes place when gas is drawn from the red giant into the smaller star, where the heat causes a massive explosion and emits huge amounts of light.

FACT FILE

Even with today's most powerful and advanced equipment, there is no visible limit to the Universe. No one is totally sure of the shape of the Universe.

WHICH PHENOMENON IS KNOWN AS A NEBULA?

A nebula is a huge cloud of white-hot gas and solid material that whirls about in interstellar space getting smaller and hotter all the time. As the gas cloud grows smaller, it throws off rings of gas. Each of these rings condenses to become a star. Based on appearance, nebulae can be divided into two broad classes: dark nebulae and bright nebulae. Dark nebulae appear as irregularly shaped black patches in the sky and blot out the light of the stars lying beyond them. Bright nebulae appear as faintly luminous, glowing surfaces; they either emit their own light or reflect the light of nearby stars.

FACT FILE

The only diffuse nebula visible to the naked eye is the beautiful Orion Nebula.

WHICH ARE THE THREE MAIN TYPES OF METEORITE?

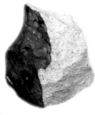

Stony meteorite

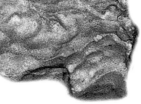

Stony iron meteorite

Iron meteorite

The three main types of meteorite. The first are called irons, which are made of an alloy (mixture) of iron and nickel. The second type, stony-irons contain rock and iron-nickel alloy. The third type are called stony meteorites and these themselves fall into three main groups: chondrites, carbonaceous chondrites and achondrites. Most meteorites are chondrites. They are made of small ball-shaped particles called chondrules, which are made of minerals that have melted and fused together. These may be the oldest rocks in the Solar System. Carbonaceous chondrites contain carbon, while achondrites are meteorites made from stone but without the spherical chondrules found in chondrites. Achondrites may be rocks blasted out of the surface of the Moon or Mars by asteroid impacts.

FACT FILE

There are a lot more meteors than usual at certain times of the year. These events are called meteor showers. Meteor showers last for anything from a few hours to several days. Some meteor showers can produce hundreds of shooting stars an hour.

WHICH ASTEROID IS THE BIGGEST?

Asteroids are chunks of rock that orbit the Sun. They are pieces of rock left over from the formation of the planets and moons. Most asteroids are too far away and too faint to be seen clearly without a telescope. Most orbit far away, beyond Mars, but occasionally one may come closer to the Sun... or Earth. Asteroids have hit the Earth in the past. A major impact about 65 million years ago may be linked to the extinction of the dinosaurs. The biggest asteroid, called Ceres, is about 933 kilometres (580 miles) across. Ceres was the first asteroid to be discovered. It was found by the Italian astronomer Giuseppe Piazzi in 1801.

FACT FILE

The 'asteroid belt' lies between the orbits of Mars and Jupiter. It is thought that this may have been the shattered remains of a planet destroyed by Jupiter's enormous gravity.

WHICH NATION LAUNCHED THE FIRST SPACE SHUTTLE?

The Americans launched the first space shuttle. Called Columbia, it went into space in 1981. A space shuttle is a re-usable spacecraft. It was developed to provide a re-usable, and therefore cheaper, vehicle for launching satellites and for other work in space. The shuttle is a bulky delta-winged aircraft with powerful rocket motors. At launch, two solid-fuel booster rockets are strapped to its sides, and a giant fuel tank is fixed to its belly. The rockets and fuel tank fall away after launch, and the rockets are recovered and re-used. In orbit, the shuttle's cargo bay opens to release satellites or allow the crew to work in space. The shuttle lands on a runway like a conventional aircraft.

FACT FILE

At takeoff the space shuttle weighs 2,000 tonnes (2,200 tons). It burns almost all of its fuel in the first few minutes after launch, then continues to coast into its orbit 300 km (185 miles) above the surface of the Earth.

WHICH NATIONS HAVE SPACE STATIONS?

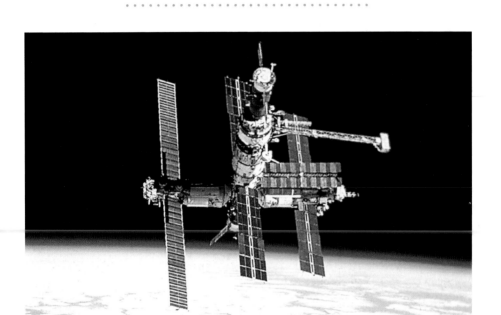

Although the Americans put the first station in space, many nations have contributed to them. The Russians have the Mir Space Station and have also contributed to the International Space Station, along with many European nations, the US and Japan. Space stations allow the crew to work in space for long periods in conditions of zero gravity. While conditions in space capsules and the space shuttle are cramped, space stations are more suitable for longer stays in space. Rockets or the space shuttle bring supplies of air and food to the space station, and often a replacement crew. Space stations are constructed from modules that are small enough to be carried by rockets or the space shuttle, which are assembled once they are in orbit.

FACT FILE

Skylab was the first US space station. One of its tasks was to test how humans behaved in microgravity.